THE
DEPRESSION
RELIEF
WORKBOOK

6 WEEKS TO A HAPPIER YOU

MELODY R. GREEN

The Depression Relief Workbook:
6 weeks to a happier you

PLEASE NOTE:

The Depression Relief Workbook is intended for general information purposes only and is not intended to replace medical advice or treatment. If you are dealing with any sort of physical, mental or emotional disorders, we suggest you consult your physician or therapist and use the exercises in this book under their supervision. Neither the author nor the publisher assumes any responsibility for your improper use of this book.

Any application of the material outlined in the following pages is at the reader's discretion and is his or her sole responsibility. These techniques are not designed to replace medical or mental health procedures but as support only. All names used in examples have been changed to protect the privacy of the individuals.

Published by: LULU Publishing Services

ISBN: 978-171636-490-7

Dedication

To you.

To the "you" that's feeling lost; overwhelmed, darkly dead inside, switched off from life, wondering why you should be even considering picking this workbook up and trying yet again to come out from under the dark, wet blankets of depression or the hyperventilating breaths of anxiety.

I see you. I get you. I've been like you and I'm here to share with you a big secret.

You are brave, daring and have courage beyond the dis-ease of your depression and anxiety and…

I love you for it.

Praise for The Depression Relief Workbook

"As Melody states upfront in this remarkable work: "Mental health is a multifaceted issue that often needs to take a multi-levelled approach." Her latest publication, The Depression Relief Workbook, is an example of that multi-levelled approach to understanding, owning, and then healing depression and anxiety. A helpful combination of theory and practice is offered throughout the book, making it a comprehensive yet accessible tool for the reader. At the right times, Melody shares bite-sized experiences of her own mental health journey, making her a credible guide who aims to inspire with authenticity and integrity. True to her belief that our mental health deserves a multi-levelled approach, this workbook is an invitation to explore a more (secular) spiritually-based approach to wellbeing. This may well be the missing piece of your mental wellbeing puzzle.

It also makes this book particularly helpful to those of us who identify as healers, empaths and highly sensitive to people, places and events. Melody helps you understand your unique skills set better and shares an abundance of practical tools to enhance your mental, emotional, physical and spiritual health. The Depression Relief Workbook also includes a beautiful audio album to accompany some of the activities, as well as links to other helpful resources. Another testament to Melody's commitment to offering high-quality holistic support during and long after you have completed your workbook."

- Christoph Spiessens - Christoph Spiessens Coaching Solutions Ltd.
www.ChristophSpiessens.com

"I absolutely love the workbook. I feel that you explain depression, symptoms and causes extremely clearly and factually. I particularly loved Chapter 5 around the topic of loneliness and that you have brought in modern-day factors such as Covid19 and social isolation.

The weekly workbooks are great – clear, simple but detailed and I can see the difference having this focus means over time. Love, love it!! THANK YOU!"

- Sean, UK

"Tools I could follow easily. They've given me hope."

- Carly, NSW, Australia

"THANK YOU! Thank you! I can't begin to tell you how much difference your workbook has made to me!"

- Julie, Victoria, Australia

"This workbook was life-changing - Highly recommended."

- Michelle, Sydney, Australia

"Sometimes it's hard not to think you are totally on your own and no one has ever gone through the same as you, So firstly, I want to thank you for sharing your personal story with us, the reader. But then you give options, lots of tools, music tracks and workbooks, and instead of feeling overwhelmed, I feel like I have a path to follow through the rabbit hole I've fallen into. You've given me a way to get out, a lifeline. Thank you! You are an angel."

- Matt, ACT, Australia

Heartfelt thanks to...

No one reaches optimum emotional and mental wellbeing without the assistance of many people; be that therapists, counsellors, friends, family or others.

To be really heard, acknowledged and accepted is powerful soul medicine that unfortunately, too many of us have not received in our lives. The results are found in the many statistics that form mental illness and disorders.

I would like to thank the many, many helpers, aides, therapists, shamans, healers, wise women and teachers who I've met along my journey…
You are all magnificent, and I would not be here without you.

I would also like to thank my many clients…

You are resilient, wise warriors battling the last frontiers of human self-understanding. I salute your courage, wisdom and the multitude of gifts your unhappiness shields from you. I hope I've helped you uncover those gifts and you are using them to bring you more joy and happiness than you've known previously.

Ultimately, we are all here to experience love.

I am deeply grateful for how full my cup of love has been this lifetime.

About the Author

Melody R. Green is the Happy Life Mentor, award-winning author, and qualified career adviser to women.

Her desire to create tools to assist in self-actualisation led her to become an Aura-Soma and flower essence therapist; she also hosted a weekly radio show on conscious creating called Creative Soul Cafe Radio Show, with over one million listeners weekly!

Melody developed these practical techniques to help deal with challenging people, events and emotional situations so she could function in the world as an HSP (highly sensitive person) and empath. Now it's time to share these techniques with others.

She leads the field in emotional well-being and her accomplishments include being a:
- Colour and sound therapist
- Flower essence therapist
- Energy healer and teacher
- Career coach
- Soul coach
- Angel communicator
- Helping people in transition to understand their emotions better

She has advised more than a million young people, men and women between 14 and 64 on career options for Australian Government agencies for 12 years. She spent 15 years as a professional singer and 18 years as an Energy Healer, Soul Coach and Intuitive Counsellor.

Melody has been nominated twice for the Telstra Business Women of the Year Awards for her work in the community working with young people and also senior Australians.

Her book, Your Career Your Way - the Workbook, was nominated for the International Authors Network Book of the Year Awards in 2015 - Non-Fiction Business Category.

Her journey has given her insight into what it is to have boundary issues in relationships and she's overcome depression and maintained her emotional balance using these techniques.

She has helped hundreds of people find their emotional equilibrium using her programs.

Here are some other interesting things to know about Melody R. Green:
- She loves flowers. They are her "go to" when she's feeling blue or happy or anytime in between!
- She collects china cups, saucers and teapots, and so of course, afternoon tea is her favourite meal of the day and her favourite tea is chai.
- Melody was a professional singer in her twenties. She sang classical, opera, jazz and cabaret, and founded an opera company in her spare time!
- She was born 11 minutes before her twin brother.
- Her Western Astrology Sign - Scorpio ~ Chinese Astrology Sign - Monkey ~ Numerology number – 11.
- She loves music, particularly world music, Bach and instrumental guitar, flute, oboe and harp.
- And of course, she loves colour because bursting colour all around her makes her feel alive and joyful!

She's been tested in her life by:
- Depression
- Sexual abuse
- Loss of her twin brother
- Divorce and sole parenting

Melody is an expert in creating tools and techniques that work for emotional well-being. She will help you to feel happy and safe in a crisis so you can do your job effectively and not feel emotionally exhausted or worse at the end of the day!

Melody lives in Sydney, NSW, Australia.

Other books by Melody R. Green

Emotional Survival Guide
A Tipsy Man Goes Naked – Love Tales and Recipes
Beloved, I Love You So...
Your Career Your Way
132 Career Tips for Women
Blessings Vol. 1
The Art of Flirting and Seduction
Soul Talk
The Angels' Gratitude Diary
The Angels' Blessings Journal

Colour Medicine Cards – due out December 2020

Did you know?
Melody is currently writing her first novel! For more information, please check out her website.

How to get in touch with Melody
You may find details on Melody at www.melodyrgreen.com and www.melodyrgreenbooks.com

Book a consultation with Melody
To book a consultation with Melody, please contact her at: thedepressionreliefworkbook@gmail.com

Contents

WEEK #2 - SMELL AND AROMAS - Days 8-14
- Preparation
- Emotions and aroma
- Progress Diary and Exercises
- The soundtrack for the sense of smell
- Integration and Weekly Review

WEEK #3 - TASTE AND FLAVOURS - Days 15-21
- Preparation
- Emotions and flavours
- Progress Diary and Exercises
- The soundtrack for the sense of taste
- Integration and Weekly Review

WEEK #4 - HEARING AND SOUNDS - Days 22-28
- Preparation
- Emotions and sounds
- Progress Diary and Exercises
- The soundtrack for the sense of hearing
- Integration and Weekly Review

WEEK #5 - TOUCH - GIVING AND RECEIVING - Days 29-35
- Preparation
- Emotions and giving and receiving touch
- Progress Diary and Exercises
- The soundtrack for the sense of touch
- Integration and Weekly Review

WEEK #6 - FEELING AND EMOTIONS - Days 36-42
- Preparation
- Emotions and feelings
- Progress Diary and Exercises
- The soundtrack for the sense of feeling
- Integration and Weekly Review

Chapter 13 - Resources

Foreword

Having just reviewed Melody's *The Depression Relief Workbook*, I have to say she has really hit the mark. We often hear of depression and anxiety and the impacts of this in mainstream medicine, and the gift here is the connection Melody has made to complementary therapies and how they can support us to come back from the darkest of places.

Having experienced depression and anxiety, I can relate to the exercises in the workbook and the benefits of same. I have spent many years working in health and complementary therapies and I am a registered nurse, intuitive coach, speaker, and published author. I truly value the journey back to self.

Melody takes you on this journey, embracing modalities that can support you and she can assist you with that reconnection that you may have lost. Melody highlights the necessity of this connection and it is with this in mind that I'd encourage you to invest and immerse yourself into this unique journey. You will learn so much about yourself and the innate tools that you have and may have forgotten. You will also bridge the gap between any such diagnosis and your holistic health. Herein lies the gift.

Melody is a compassionate, professional and inspiring woman who has made it her mission to support and empower each individual, gently guiding them to their spirit/soul essence. Diagnosis is one thing but lived experience is another, and the only way to the self is through a gentle yet powerful program such as this. Melody is more than happy to work in combination with your doctor, psychologist or therapist, if this is what you choose.

You will not be disappointed with the direction and guidance provided. Know that self-awareness is key to health improvement and as you connect with yourself, you will begin to feel the cloud lifting and/or the worries subsiding.

Thank you, Melody, for bringing the necessary components together, providing your clients with the best opportunity for their mental and emotional wellbeing. Ultimately, this program is the culmination of all the tools necessary for the balancing of body, heart, mind and spirit.

Robyn Ridley - Intuitive Coach, Speaker and Published Award-Winning Author - www.RobynRidley.com

This book has a series of worksheets, workbooks, quizzes and Mp3's. All of them are found on my website at the following link:
www.melodyrgreenbooks.com

CHAPTER 1

* * * * *

So you've bought the workbook - Now what?

Firstly, congratulations! It takes courage to get here. You've bought this workbook because you recognise you are struggling to maintain your emotional equilibrium. You have found yourself in a period of time where you have been feeling down, possibly depressed, and feel you need help to get out of this cycle.

You could have already taken the step to see your doctor, counsellor or practitioner but you want to do more for yourself. You are hopeful that what is included in this book will help you.

Just sit in this feeling for a moment… you are hopeful. This is a different emotion to feeling depressed. It is you fighting back and saying you deserve more than the darkness that you know so well. It is you looking for the light, searching for the end of the tunnel, and it's a start. Well done. Take full credit for your actions.

Recovery from depression or depressed emotional states of being does not happen in a flash. It is not a fast, direct route such as an arrow to a bullseye, but rather a slow, step by step, one foot in front of the other journey to wellness. It takes time and patience.

One of the most wonderful things I've seen with clients I've worked with who have depression or anxiety is their capacity to feel. I encourage you to see your sensitivity and capacity to feel as your super sauce rather than your kryptonite. You came into this world to experience life – all of it – and you know at a deep, possibly unrecognised part of yourself that this emotional sensitivity holds gifts for you. The work you have done, the work you are doing and what you may do in the future is all part of your unique way of looking at the world... and guess what? We need you desperately and unequivocally. Don't give up and don't hide your beautiful self.

What's in the workbook?
A combination of information, exercises, meditations and visualisations, quizzes and worksheets every week for 6 weeks, plus an album of music to go hand in hand with the work.

What's covered?
- Positive Learning
- Clearing Negativity
- Dealing with Loneliness and Isolation
- Sight and Colours
- Smell and Aromas
- Taste and Flavours
- Hearing and Sounds
- Touch – Giving and Receiving
- Feelings and Emotions

How long does it take?
1-3 days of preparation.
6 weeks of *The Depression Relief Workbook* and exercises.
1 day review.

How often do I have to use it?
You may find that you need to use this workbook more than once, especially if you have been feeling depressed for a long time. These exercises are to help you connect with your senses and appreciate the life you are living right now.

The techniques, meditations and worksheets are to help you set up a self-care program that over time will result in a better frame of mind. And I would hope that if you find yourself having future episodes of depression that you come back to these tools to help you again, as they are designed to be used in this manner.

What can you expect to happen?
- Techniques you can use indefinitely and for as long as necessary.
- New understanding of how your senses and your emotions work.
- New vocabulary to express your emotions.
- Incremental shifts and changes in mood that show you are moving forward.
- A lifting of your spirits.

If I use this workbook, does that mean that I don't have to go to my counsellor, psychologist or therapist?
- At no point in the use of this workbook is it suggested that you change your current regime to handle your depression.
- You are strongly supported to continue your work with a counsellor, psychologist, therapist or doctor.
- It is not suggested that you come off medication. This is a matter for you and your doctor or medical practitioner to decide.
- The tools in this workbook are to support you in the choices you make about how you navigate your day. They are designed to help you understand your emotions more and give you tools and techniques that assist you to strengthen the connection between your senses and your emotions.
- I have worked with many clients who have found it helpful to be aware of their senses, to learn to appreciate the day they have in front of them and to become aware of the flexibility and fluctuation of their emotions. They have found that these exercises give them hope and a feeling of centred-ness and serenity when they are anxious. I hope that you will have the same results by using this workbook.

CHAPTER 2

* * * * *

Why I developed the Depression Relief Workbook

As you can see, depression is a complex and multi-faceted disorder that to my mind required a holistic approach.

My work as a colour therapist opened my eyes to the interconnection of the mind, body, heart and spirit. What I had instinctively known was given a foundation to sit on. I learned about the endocrine system and the impact of colour. These things I felt I knew but did not have the language to explain, and with this knowledge, I began to ask questions about my emotions and how my body coped with depression. I began to use colour to treat my emotions and find colour supported me in ways that talking with a counsellor had not. I could use colour to build and transform my energy when it was depleted and throughout, I used myself as the guinea pig and I studied my emotional and mental responses to colour.

As I worked with colour as a therapy, I realised there was a spiritual component to depression that had not come to the surface when I spoke to counsellors. It was an "aha" moment for me to make the realisation that my spirit and soul had not been included in my life choices and what I was doing in my life.

The question I kept returning to was:

What if depression is a sign I am disconnected from my soul self and the disconnection from life and others is merely a symptom of that primary disconnection?

This question did not leave me but grew to a point that I decided to approach my depression from this premise and see what happened. Day by day, I started to feel better. It was slow but there was progress and I felt that I could handle a broader array of emotional responses. I started to re-frame "being depressed" into "being disconnected". What this reframing did was give me more opportunity to explore my emotions without being limited to the label called depression.

What I wanted to find out was - How could I reconnect and what did I need to know about my spirit, my real being, my soul self?

As is the way with Spirit when we start finding answers for our issues, Spirit sends us clients with the same problems, so the wisdom can be passed on. My clients started to feel better. Some had incremental changes while others had massive 90-degree shifts in thinking and handling their depression.

And to this day, even if my clients come to me for very different reasons, at some level, we will need to go back to a time where they felt depressed or anxious to a point that it blocked their ability to properly function in their life.

∞

This workbook has taken many years to put together. It has happened via trial and error as I went through my journey and helped out my clients as part of their healing journey.

I didn't wake up one morning and decide that this was THE book I wanted to write, although I did wake up after my 40th birthday and decide I wanted to be a published author – that's another story!

I have been working with various editions of this workbook as a program I use with my clients. Again, it is not that I have advertised this work in the past but it is there for my clients as they need.

I have been very reluctant to write a book on this work as I am not a trained psychologist or psychiatrist and have found when I have worked with clients who have their own health professionals, those professionals are often aggressively dismissive of the work I do.

Occasionally I am contacted by a professional in the psych field who is curious to see who I am and what I do because they've noticed marked improvements in their clients, but I am quick to point out that these are tools I've developed to support their ongoing work with the mental health professionals and I am not in competition with them, nor would I suggest my clients stop their work with the said professional or the treatment prescribed.

The Depression Relief Workbook is not a cure. It is a tool of activities to support your mental health awareness. Having said that, I have never had a client who has not benefited by these tools, providing they have used them consistently and properly and are willing to be curious about how they respond to them. Clients who do the Daily Check-In, for example, find that on days they forget, they are more likely to get into emotional slumps. While on days they use the tool properly, they can maintain a better state of wellbeing and can pinpoint when the problem arises. This is valuable information and awareness to have when it is so easy to label your emotions via a short cut and then give up finding a way to express and experience the overwhelming emotional response of a bad day.

Mental health is a multifaceted issue that often needs to take a multi-levelled approach. I hope you will see these tools as a way to assist you to manage your emotions more healthily, allowing you to enjoy your days more and feel more fulfilment in your life.

My Story
I was born a twin in the mid-1950s in the U.K. My family said that all childhood illnesses came into the house with my brother and once I got the illness, I would have the serious dose lasting many days and he would be up and well within a couple of days, running around like normal. Every year without fail, through the autumn or winter, I would find myself in bed, off school with a severe case of bronchitis, and some years maybe more than one dose. These were tedious and difficult times for me as I loved school and learning. When I was nearly nine years old, we migrated to New Zealand and I attended nine different schools during my school years. As a result, I found keeping friends a challenge and was ostracised by students and teachers alike, because of the way I spoke and conducted myself. As an act of self-preservation, I learned

early to keep to myself. I was an imaginative child and books were my great joy. Later, this imagination would be added to a singing talent that was far more developed than my parents had ever anticipated, and I took part in many singing competitions and productions in my teens, moving into a semi-professional singing career by the time I was 18. During my teens, my mother would comment that I was the moody and dramatic one of the family, that I had moods. Later in my teens, I could tell that my moods were highly impacted by my hormones and there was a cycle of being UP when things were going well – usually connected to when I was working in a show and DOWN when I was not. These cycles happened every 8-12 weeks generally, which is the production cycle of a theatrical show.

I did not consider this as being depressed. I considered this as being a creative person and performer. My singing career took me to Sydney, Australia, for what I thought would be about a five year period before heading off to Europe. These plans did not eventuate. It was some years later that a counsellor would point out the pattern to me. At 29, having tried for many years to have a professional fulltime career as a singer and having spent seven years building an opera company from scratch, help-ing many others (singers, musicians, backstage staff, etc.) get their career start in the industry, I finally decided to stop fighting for a professional singing career and put my talents elsewhere.

Now depression truly arrived. I consider the following 3 years "the dark night of my soul". Everything started to come to a head at that time, creating a healing crisis because I could no longer think that everything was ok. I had stopped long enough to see some serious issues needed healing, including the loss of my singing career dreams, the sexual abuse from my late teens that had not been properly addressed, and the trauma of arriving in a new country again with no support systems in place, no job and little financial backing. These issues would surface over again as is wont to do with trauma and emotions that are suppressed.

As I threw myself into a new career of sales and marketing, I felt the real work needed to be done on the sexual abuse that was impacting on how I conducted myself in relationships. My hormonal clock was ticking and I decided I needed to find a partner, settle down and have children if I was not going to have a singing career.

7

So began an intensive time of counselling and therapy for over a year, after which I felt I had overcome my experiences and could move forward into a settled permanent relationship.

Indeed, I married at 33 and had a child at 35. It was a difficult time of adjustment, not helped by a child who suffered from colic, who slept only 45 minutes at a time, and a husband who was on night shift hours and no family support to ease the burden because both my husband and I were migrants to Australia. I was exhausted, sleep-deprived, resentful and not coping with, nor interested in my home, instead of spending all my time focusing on looking after my son.

I had gone from having a job as an ESL teacher within a vibrant school community of work colleagues and activities that supported my sense of self to a home that was surviving on one income. My husband had many friends from his culture and could spend time with them in between work but I was too exhausted to have the same break, and my friends were single and understandably disinterested in talking about babies, bodily functions and sleep deprivation! As I had little time to read, watch the news or generally function as a mature and interesting adult, I had very little to say to my single friends and it felt unrewarding to keep making coffee dates with them. Anyone who has been the main carer for a young infant will tell you that looking after a screaming infant almost 24/7 is no picnic, and to add to the despair was a relationship that was starting to show cracks because we had not had sufficient time to work through our cultural differences, the expectations of our roles as partners, never mind parents, and to top it off, my husband started a multi-level marketing business that he expected me to do most of the work in... and it was this business that became the final straw.

After a couple of years of trying to find common ground with my son's father and my son still not sleeping through the night (he didn't do this until he was five and a half years old) I finally plucked up enough courage to leave the marriage. I'd been married seven years, my son was four and a half years old and I was a functioning depressive. Stoically working, raising my son and dealing with my stuff as and when I could. By this time, I realised I was depressed and needed help. I chose not to go the medical route. My reasoning was two-fold. Firstly, just after I was sexually abused, I was billeted with a woman who had a husband, two children and suffered depression. She was treated with anti-depressants and I watched her become addicted to the drug and lose her creative mojo. This experience had a profound impact on me and I felt that having stopped smoking with difficulty some ten years earlier (and after three attempts), plus having an eating disorder, I might be considered a high-risk addictive personality and I did not wish to be in that condition for my son.

So I went the alternative route. I moved to a more nutritious vegetarian diet. As I no longer smoked or drank alcohol, I started working with a kinesiologist to work out why my hormones were so rampant and what emotional trauma was still captured in my body. It was a slow process and there were plenty of emotional traumas to choose from. Over the next 2-3 years, I worked on many levels of the trauma and uncovered much that explained why I might have a depressive nature. Throughout this work, I went through the divorce, child custody battles, early menopause, unproductive dates with unsuitable men and a period of isolation. As a result, I clawed my way out of the level of depression I had experienced during my postpartum days but I never seemed to fully stabilise my emotions until I started to work with mindfulness and read fascinating information about being an empath.

By this time, I was working in the alternative health and wellbeing sector as a colour therapist and could, with the use of colour and flower essences, rebalance my emotions quicker than ever before.

The most important piece of my research though was the information about being an empath. This was the missing piece of the puzzle for me. I had begun to journal my emotions and noticed a few things:

1) When I was around certain people, my energy dropped.
2) I could go to a shopping mall quite upbeat and energised and within 30 minutes, I was dragging myself around as though I'd been working hard for a whole day.
3) Subtle shifts in my mood were being affected by the moon cycles.
4) My bio-rhythms also seemed to play a part in my mood swings.

NB: If you have never completed an exercise to diary your moods, I would urge you to do this – it will be an enlightening experience for you.

9

Understanding my empathy, which made me so good at my profession, also allowed me to see that more than 70% of my emotions did not even belong to me. As an empath, I strongly felt the need to help others. I am particularly tuned to feeling people's pain, especially their emotions and thoughts. These aspects of humanity are felt as energy and as I had found out through colour therapy impacted on the endocrine system, which in turn changes the neurological transmitters of information to the brain and impacts on the happiness hormones of serotonin, dopamine, oxytocin and endorphins. Your hormones and neurotransmitters are involved in lots of essential processes like heart rate, stress levels, digestion, moods and feelings.

Briefly, these hormones are responsible for different aspects of emotional health and wellbeing.

Dopamine: pleasure, motivation
Serotonin: wellbeing, happiness, mood stabilising
Endorphins: relaxation, pain relief, the runner's high
Oxytocin: bonding, trust and love in relationships

Finally, I had found all the parts of the puzzle. Now all I needed to do was work out how I could make them work together harmoniously so I could be in charge of my emotions, rather than have them in charge of me. The next few years were spent in discovering this, firstly with me and then my clients, until some years later, *The Depression Relief Program* was born.

CHAPTER 3

* * * * *

Defining Depression and Anxiety

Depression affects how people feel about themselves. They may lose interest in work, hobbies and doing things they normally enjoy.

They may lack energy, have difficulty sleeping or sleep more than usual. Some people feel irritable and some find it hard to concentrate. Depression makes life more difficult to manage from day-to-day.

What are the symptoms of depression?
A person may be depressed if, for more than two weeks, they have felt sad, down or miserable most of the time or has lost interest or pleasure in usual activities, and have also experienced several of the signs and symptoms across at least three of the categories below.

NB: Not everyone will experience all of these symptoms all of the time nor will it be true if someone is experiencing some of these symptoms that they are depressed. This is why it's worth speaking to your doctor or a counsellor if you notice a change in your behaviour, feelings or thoughts.

Behaviour
- not going out anymore
- not getting things done at work or school
- withdrawing from close family and friends
- relying on alcohol and sedatives
- not engaging in usually enjoyable activities
- not being able to concentrate

Feelings

- overwhelmed
- guilty
- irritable
- frustrated
- lacking in confidence
- unhappy
- indecisive
- disappointed
- miserable
- sad

Thoughts

- 'I'm a failure.'
- 'It's my fault.'
- 'Nothing good ever happens to me.'
- 'I'm worthless.'
- 'Life's not worth living.'
- 'People would be better off without me.'

Physical

- constantly tired
- sick and run down
- headaches and muscle pains
- churning gut
- sleep problems
- loss or change of appetite
- significant weight loss or gain

What kind of depression types are there?

Like everything about depression and anxiety, it is not straight forward. Situations may trigger trauma from childhood that creates longer, more serious bouts of depression or anxiety. But for this discussion, here are the most common.

1) Life events or Situational Depression or Anxiety

Research suggests that continuing and on-going difficulties such as:

- long-term unemployment
- living in an abusive or uncaring relationship
- long-term isolation or loneliness
- financial stress
- drug or alcohol addiction

will impact on a person's ability to deal with depression and anxiety long term, especially if the person is already at risk of depression because they've had past experiences.

2) Personal factors

- Family history – Depression can run in families and some people will be at an increased genetic risk. However, this doesn't mean that a person will automatically experience depression if a parent or close relative has had the condition. Life circumstances and other personal factors are still likely to have an important influence.
- Personality – Some people may be more at risk of depression because of their personality, particularly if they tend to worry a lot, have low self-esteem, are perfectionists, are sensitive to personal criticism, or are self-critical and negative.
- Serious medical illness – Having a medical illness can trigger depression in two ways. Serious illnesses can bring about depression directly or can contribute to depression through associated stress and worry, especially if it involves long-term management of the illness and/or chronic pain.
- Drug and alcohol use – Drug and alcohol use can both lead to and result from depression. Many people with depression also have drug and alcohol problems. Over 500,000 Australians will experience depression and a substance use disorder at the same time, at some point in their lives.

3) Changes in the brain

- Although there has been a lot of research in this complex area, there is still much that we do not know. Depression is not simply the result of a 'chemical imbalance', for example, because a person has too much or not enough of a particular brain chemical. There are many and multiple causes of depression.

- It's important to note that a person can't always identify the cause of depression or change difficult circumstances. The most important thing is to recognise the signs and symptoms and seek help.
- There are different types of depression. Symptoms can range from relatively minor (but still disabling) through to very severe, so it is helpful to be aware of the range of disorders and their specific symptoms.

4) Major depression

- **Major depression** is sometimes called Major Depressive Disorder, clinical depression, unipolar depression or simply depression. It involves low mood and/or loss of interest and pleasure in usual activities. The symptoms are experienced most days and last for at least two weeks. The symptoms interfere with all areas of a person's life, including work and social relationships.
- **Depression** is often described in terms of severity (mild, moderate or severe) and sometimes according to the type of depression (melancholic or psychotic).
- **Melancholia** is the term used to describe a severe form of depression where many of the physical symptoms of depression are present. One of the major changes is that the person can be observed to move more slowly. The person is also more likely to have a depressed mood that is characterised by complete loss of pleasure in everything, or almost everything.
- **Psychotic depression:** Sometimes people affected by depression can lose touch with reality and experience psychosis. This can involve hallucinations (for example, seeing or hearing things that are not there) or delusions (false beliefs that are not shared by others), such as believing they are bad or evil, or that they are being watched or followed. They can also be paranoid, feeling as though everyone is against them or that they are the cause of illness or bad events occurring around them.
- **Antenatal and postnatal depression:** Women are at an increased risk of depression during pregnancy (known as the antenatal or prenatal period) and in the year following childbirth

14

(known as the postnatal period). You may also come across the term 'perinatal', which describes the period covered by pregnancy and the first year after the baby's birth. The causes of depression at this time can be complex and are often the result of a combination of factors. In the days immediately following birth, many women experience the 'baby blues', which is a common condition related to hormonal changes, affecting up to 80 per cent of women. The 'baby blues', as well as general stress adjusting to pregnancy and/or a new baby, are common experiences but are different from depression. Depression is longer-lasting and can affect not only the mother but her relationship with her baby, the child's development, and the mother's relationship with her partner and with other members of the family. Almost 10 per cent of women will experience depression during pregnancy. This increases to 16 per cent in the first three months after having a baby.

- **Bipolar disorder** used to be known as 'manic depression' because the person experiences periods of mania in addition to periods of depression, with periods of normal mood in between. Nine mania symptoms include feeling great, having lots of energy, having racing thoughts and little need for sleep, talking fast, having difficulty focusing on tasks, and feeling frustrated and irritable. This is not just a fleeting experience. Sometimes the person loses touch with reality and has episodes of psychosis. Experiencing psychosis involves hallucinations (for example seeing or hearing something that is not there) or having delusions (e.g. the person believing they have superpowers).

- **Persistent depressive disorder (dysthymia)** the symptoms of dysthymia are similar to those of major depression but are less severe. However, in the case of dysthymia, symptoms last longer. A person has to have this milder depression for more than two years to be diagnosed with dysthymia.

- **Seasonal affective disorder (SAD)** is a mood disorder that has a seasonal pattern. The cause of the disorder is unclear; however, it is thought to be related to the variation in light exposure in different seasons. It's characterised by mood disturbances (either an episode of depression or mania) that begin and end in a particular season. Depression that starts in winter and subsides when the season ends is the most common. SAD is usually diagnosed after the person has had the same symptoms during the same specific period or season for a couple of years. People with seasonal affective disorder depression are more likely to experience lack of energy, sleep too much, overeat, gain weight and crave carbohydrates.

What is anxiety? – A definition
The symptoms of anxiety conditions are sometimes not all that obvious as they often develop slowly over time and, given we all experience some anxiety at various points in our lives, it can be hard to know how much is too much.

Normal anxiety tends to be limited in time and connected with some stressful situation or event, such as a job interview. The type of anxiety experienced by people with an anxiety condition is more frequent or persistent, not always connected to an obvious challenge, and impacts on their quality of life and day-to-day functioning.

What are the symptoms of anxiety?
These are just some of several symptoms that you might experience. They're not designed to provide a diagnosis – for that you'll need to see a doctor – but they can be used as a guide.

While each anxiety condition has its unique features, there are some common symptoms, including:

Physical:
- panic attacks
- hot and cold flushes
- racing heart
- tightening of the chest
- quick or irregular breathing,
- restlessness, or feeling tense
- wound up and edgy

Psychological:
- excessive fear

- worry
- catastrophizing
- obsessive thinking

Mental:
- short-term memory loss
- inability to grasp or follow directions

Behavioural:
- avoidance of situations that make you feel anxious, which can impact on study, work or social life
- anxious and fretful around large numbers of people gathering

Anxiety and Handling Potential Threats

While depression is usually centred in past conditions, threats and feelings, anxiety is most often about future probabilities, so handling potential threats must be part of the self-care resilience building for someone who suffers from anxiety.

In 2020, we cannot deny the elephant in the room – COVID-19. While for some, this has been a dire real-life threat or trauma to themselves or their families, for most of the population, it is a perceived, potential threat.

Responses to this threat are:
- becoming emotionally numb
- detachment
- overwhelm
- hopelessness
- overly fatigued
- blocking feelings
- information overload
- sensual overload
- lack of motivation
- feeling depressed
- helplessness
- uncertainty

- faulty decision making
- lack of commitment
- unwillingness to make decisions or act
- stymies in creative problem solving
- pessimism

When a negative situation is fantasised or worried by the mind, it can become a far greater threat than the real threat itself. Ruminating on something that is only a potential threat activates the adrenal glands to fight, flee or freeze, and as you are dealing with only a potential threat, then the most common reaction is to freeze or become immobile.

Chronic negative rumination becomes worry that results in a period of anxiety followed by depression. It matters not to the mind if the threat is real, potential, or imagined. Prolonged rumination harms mental and emotional wellbeing.

Exercise # 1 - How to break this pattern: This exercise is in Chapter Summaries at www.melodyrgreenbooks.com

What are the most common treatments for Depression and Anxiety?
I will list here but please research these treatments for yourself.

1) Psychological treatments for Depression and Anxiety – Talking therapies
- Cognitive Behaviour Therapy (CBT)
- Interpersonal Therapy (IPT)
- Behaviour Therapy (BT)
- Mindfulness-based Cognitive Therapy (MBCT)

2) Medical treatments for Depression and Anxiety
- Anti-depressants
- Mood stabilisers
- Anti-psychotic drugs

All of which must be prescribed by a doctor or psychiatrist and are used dependent on the severity of the problem and often prescribed in tandem with psychological treatments.

3) Alternative therapies for Depression and Anxiety

In this category, there are as many options as there are alternative treatments, however, the most common are:

- Acupuncture
- Dietary support
- Vitamins and minerals therapy
- Flower Essence Therapy
- Aromatherapy
- Meridian Tapping
- Kinesiology
- Massage
- Meditation
- Osteopathy
- Pet Therapy
- Bowen Therapy
- Colour Therapy
- Traditional Chinese Medicine

NB: Everyone is an individual and you will find that what suits someone else may not suit you. You will need to research yourself to find out what best suits you… and also which combination of treatments is best for you.

Does culture have an impact on mental health?

There are four main ways in which culture can impact on mental health. (This is not a conclusive list, as each culture will have its social parameters when dealing with depression and anxiety.)

1) Cultural stigma. Many cultures see mental health challenges as a weakness, something to be ashamed of and to hide from others. This makes it harder for sufferers to speak openly or seek treatment.

2) Understanding the symptoms. Different cultures have different ways of describing and feeling about their symptoms.

3) Community support. Cultural factors can determine how much support someone gets from their family and community when it comes to mental health. Because of the existing stigma, minorities are sometimes left to find mental health treatment and support alone.

4) Resources. When looking for mental health treatment, you want to talk to someone who understands your specific experiences and concerns. It can sometimes be difficult or time-consuming to find resources and treatment options that take into account specific cultures' factors and needs.

New developments through neuroscience
While neuroscience is still in its infancy as a scientific discipline, there have been some excellent breakthroughs around understanding how the brain, hormones and emotions work, some of which are supporting the metaphysical and spiritual precepts and the importance of holistic approaches to depression.

Jill Bolte Taylor, a noted neuroscientist working with mindfulness and emotions, says:
"An emotion only lasts 1.5 minutes by itself (without the fuel of our thoughts)."

So why are we holding onto emotions and letting our minds play over the same old tapes, rather than allowing our emotions to flow with ease and grace?

Are you depressed or anxious?
Beyond Blue (www.beyondblue.org.au) is an organisation that works with people who are depressed or anxious. Their website has a lot of information available on it and is a very good resource for sufferers.

The FACTS and FIGURES of Depression

How many people get depressed in their lifetime?
The World Health Organization has suggested that the number is 1 in 4 people, for their lifetime. Some people will have more than one episode. These figures were before COVID-19, which has caused so much fear, anxiety and depression due to the uncertainty of the situation, fear of death from the virus, isolation and social distancing.

In simple terms, if you are more predisposed to extraversion than introversion, you may find the COVID-19 restrictions hard to live by. If you're more introverted, you might find the isolation supportive and enjoyable.

My personal experience

I advertise my services on a therapy site. I have been on this site since February 2020 – here are the results of enquiries for counselling services during the year.

2020	March 2020	May 2020	August 2020	October 2020
10-15 per day across the country	COVID-19 Lockdown initiated	25-35 per day across the country	50-60 per day across the country	80-90 per day across the country

These figures are alarming for the following reasons:

- 8-9 times the number of people seeking help since March (i.e. in 8 months).
- This number reflects people who are aware they are suffering and seeking help, versus those who need help and are not seeking it.
- Increased unemployment, financial stress, social insecurity and isolation are key contributors to suicide among men (teenagers and older).
- Between 1950 and 1990, the suicide rates in Australian men increased from 13.7 deaths per 100,000 to 20.7 deaths, at which time, the Government began to educate the population about mental health. In the same period, the rate for suicide in women was 4.7 deaths per 100,000 to 5.2 deaths per 100,000 in 1990. These figures did not include deaths by a car accident or other 'accidents' that could have been caused by poor judgment as a result of mental health. The largest number of men suiciding in this period were men in the 15-54 years old group, whereas this number for women stretched across 15-64 age groups.
- The highest recorded rates of suicides among men are in Lithuania, with 61.3 per 100,000 deaths, while the highest recorded rates of suicide among women is in South Korea, with 22.1 per 100,000 deaths (as at 2006).
- The lowest recorded rates for both men and women were in Iran, at 0.3 per 100,000 deaths and 0.1 per 100,000 deaths respectively.

Suicide Rates across the World: www.ncbi.nlm.nih.gov/pmc/articles/PMC3367275/
Australia Suicide Rates. - www.who.int/mental_health/media/austral.pdf?ua=1

CHAPTER 4

* * * * *

Is there a different way of looking at depression or anxiety?

As part of my journey with depression, I found two aspects of depression that seemed to be ignored in the help available, and it was in these hidden corners that I found the energy and tools to help manage my depression in a positive and uplifting way, which has led to a much more fulfilled and happier life.

But… it did not happen for me overnight. It took many years of watching for what happened to me and how I went from "feeling ok to the depths of depression".

What I found was missing from the research I could get my hands-on was the spiritual impact of depression, and I started looking at why some people seemed to be more prone to depression than others.

My findings were based on the observation of myself, clients and other people I met or knew around me. It was not a clinical trial.

I have always been someone who can see patterns in things and I've spent many parts of my life looking at what connects people and what motivates them.

Firstly, this was done as part of my training to be an actor and singer. I would break down the script to find out what the character thought, what others thought about the character, and various other bits of information about the time and place the story was set, for me to put together a jigsaw puzzle of the character I was studying. Always my question for any action would be – What's the motivation of my character now? Why are they doing this? What are they feeling?

While none of this seems relevant to learning about depression, I found this training became an important way of looking at individuals with depression and finding out how they experienced depression and also what were the common threads between all people who suffer depression.

My study of the spirit led me to conclude that depression is part of being a human being and it is a doorway to deeper understanding and meaning as a soul – the spirit that drives your body to have the experiences it has.

If as a soul, we have come into this incarnation to have a physical experience and collect insight into being in a body then our emotional experiences become as important to us as any other form of experience. We, as humans, are a biofeedback system of impulses and responses and our emotions are part of that mix.

Coming to this understanding was freeing because it meant that there wasn't anything wrong with me or people that suffer from depression. It was not an illness as such but a misconnection in the healthy messaging of the body's biofeedback system that may be impacted upon by being overwhelmed by too much information or being closed off from the information coming into the energy field.

My time as the daughter of a toolmaker and car mechanic gave me a sense that it was worth finding out what was wrong with the body, fix it and then treat it with regular tune-ups to keep it running at its very best. It also struck me that if I could fine-tune my receptivity to changes in my emotional and mental state I could do a lot of the work of keeping my emotions healthy, by myself.

My father once said to me, "If a car could speak to us, it would tell us much earlier than when it has broken down what's wrong with it and we could make sure it ran smoothly all its life. But instead, we wait until it's broken before treating it with the care and consideration it deserves!"

And isn't that true about how we treat our emotional and mental health? So my first decision was to look at depression from a spiritual perspective and ask why?

Why was depression a part of the human condition and what gift did the depression hold?

This is what I came up with:

1) Depression is part of a series of emotions possible for a human being to express.

2) Depression happens when one set of emotions are overworked and the emotional fluidity gets stuck (like a spring in a machine that is overused, it becomes loose and is no longer able to keep the right tension to allow the mechanism to spring back to a new setting).

3) The same emotional triggers used often enough fast track the emotions into taking a short cut that moves a person more quickly into depressive emotions that create a depressed state.

4) Once in that "emotional rut" or "low", the person suffering depression finds it harder to get out each time they go into it.

5) The less connected we are to our soul and what we as individuals have come to experience (our "why" if you will), the less meaning our lives have and the easier it is to experience depressive states.

6) The way out of our depressive states is to re-introduce meaning in incremental ways that act as footholds to climb out of the depression.

7) The way to stay out of that depressive state is to find tools that will allow you to express all your emotions but not get stuck in them.

8) Emotional and mental health comes from having a vibrant inner life or spiritual connection that ensures you feel connected to your soul mission and purpose.

9) We as humans are too quick to label our emotions and this limits our ability to flow with them and to allow them to flow through us.

10) The labels we have for our emotions are too narrow and this limits our experiences of our emotions and funnels us into being depressed.

11) Our emotional repertoire is a beautiful thing that we should embrace and enjoy, not fear and reject.

12) Hidden behind the depression is a soul with great emotional sensitivity, and this needs to be accepted and explored in its fullness.

Then some years later, as I worked through my understanding of being an empath and highly sensitive person, I realised something that would change forever how I dealt with depression for myself and others...

If you are an empath, you are wired to see pain and discomfort in others and desire to help them by taking on that pain to relieve them, to allow them the space to heal, gain a breath of time and move forward. An empath takes this energy into their own physical body and energy field and thinks that the depressed feelings belong to them when in fact, they are not the empath's at all – they are the feelings of others.

To explain more about this, imagine that you clean houses. At the beginning of the day, your clothes are clean and neat. By the end of the day, they are dirty with dust and dirt from cleaning the houses. You, your skin and hair also carry that dirt, and when you get home, the first thing you do is have a shower and put your dirty clothes to be washed.

For empaths, being around emotionally disturbed people, be that depression, anger, frustration, grief, is like collecting the dirt on their bodies and then because they don't know they are carrying this for someone else, they continue to live their lives without cleansing their energy field. So the first question an empath needs to ask is:

Is this feeling of depression (or any other emotion) mine?

Answering this question will enable you to deal with the emotions quite differently and effectively. This is the first question I ask any of my clients, and I have created a quiz that I give to clients to help them ascertain if they are an empath (see Chapter 7).

This is how the *Depression Relief Program* was born and it has helped many clients feel in control of their depression rather than have their depression control them. Depression and anxiety are whole-body illnesses, not just a mental body illness.

Often, depression is the result of a previous shock to an individual's system that has not been treated properly or fully. Invariably, it is triggered by something that has happened too fast, too soon or is too much, leading to the senses being overloaded and overwhelmed.

This overwhelms the individual's capacity to handle the situation in a whole-body way, and what results is a series of steps that result in depression or anxiety.

These are:
EVENT – SHOCK – DISCONNECTION – ISOLATION – DISASSOCIATION – PAIN – DEPRESSION OR ANXIETY

This is how it works…
1) An **event** that triggers you into **shock** (emotional, mental or physical)
2) The response to shock is to trigger an extreme survival response from your Spirit self, which **disconnects** your Spirit from your body
3) Which results in feeling **isolated**
4) Which triggers **disassociation**
5) Which results in **pain**
6) And this results in you going into **depression or anxiety**

An individual can move throughout the whole spectrum starting at the event and moving through shock, disconnection, isolation, disassociation, pain and depression while waiting anxiously for the next event OR only cycle through part of it regularly…

e.g. #1 – shock, anxiety disconnection, pain, waiting for the event, shock, etc...
e.g. #2 – event, shock, disconnection, isolation, disassociation, pain, depression on a repetitive cycle.

To make sense of a traumatic event, the mind will fixate on the loss (i.e. person, job, sense of self-esteem, career, safety, etc.) but what's really happening is…

The soul is disconnected and the loss of this connection is the "real pain".

The Emotional Biofeedback System
When we are connected to ourselves (wholly or in an integrated fashion), the biofeedback system works on many levels. The physical body's

nervous system, joints, muscles, organs, endocrine (and other systems), brain and neurological pathways work in harmony and wholeness. All connected in a multi-dimensional way – a web or matrix of energetic connections.

A shock of any kind disconnects the brain from the nervous system and the endocrine glands are the emotional biofeedback system that your senses belong to. As a result of the trauma, your senses shift down from thrive-mode to survival-mode, meaning they function in limited ways.

Every individual is wired to one sense more than another. This is the individual's core sense. If you are a musician, for example, your sense of hearing will be finally tuned. As an individual develops through life, they have a chance to experience and develop an awareness of all senses to a greater or equal degree, depending on the individual's life choices.

During trauma, this core sense continues to receive information, but because the other senses are limited, it is likely to be receiving only part of the messages and as a result, overuse, overwear, tear, experience incomplete information gathering, limited neurological pathways and limited ways to express the emotional energy, resulting in the individual going into survival default mode. To enable wholeness, the emotional palette needs to be opened and reconnected to the senses.

In the process, the individual will be opened to a greater experience of their emotions and a more sensitive responsive biofeedback system. This is what *The Depression Relief Program* does.

What is Spiritual and Emotional Wellbeing?
As human beings, we are spiritual beings who have physical experiences through the temple of our body. As such, 75% of us happens outside of our body in our spirit, heart and mind. This part of us that is not seen belongs to an electrical field of currents and neurons that is pulsing in a field around us and makes up what we commonly call the aura (as seen by Kirlian photography). Through highly complex biofeedback systems, information, sensual responses, thoughts, beliefs and emotions flow backwards and forwards through our bodies to our brain, mind, heart and soul. If you could see a human with an x-ray vision that encompassed this biofeedback system, you would see that we are a body of

light thrumming with colour signals pulsing our body and allowing us to be in form.

This extraordinary show is happening in every single being and species on the earth, including the earth itself. To be at optimum physical health, our mental, emotional and spiritual wellbeing must also be at optimum levels. We are sensory beings, responding and reacting to all that is around us. Much of this goes unnoticed by our conscious mind, but it is nevertheless happening.

If the information is a vibrational match or higher, it will pass through us without too much response, but if it is something we need to understand as part of our journey on earth, it will cling to us until we are ready to deal with it. Most dis-ease of the mind and body (the parts we are most aware of) comes about through a build-up of residue on the non-physical planes that slow the natural vibrancy of our soul and blocks our ability to move forward with ease and grace.

What you believe about yourself and your world becomes
how the world responds to you.

At some point in your evolution, you feel sufficient pain to want to change how you think and feel, and this is the beginning of your journey towards self-actualisation.

Each of us chooses how we will use our talents and gifts to be in the world, and as such, we utilise different parts of ourselves according to our strengths and weaknesses. Most of us have been taught to recognise our weaknesses and not our strengths. Because we are constantly receiving and sending out through our biofeedback system thoughts and emotions, we are highly susceptible to others' thoughts and feelings and these are constantly impacting upon us.

It is through this system that we are linked to each other. As the collective humanity, we agree to certain beliefs, truths and facts and these give our humanity structures to support our growth. You can find out a lot more about humanity's biofeedback system and how to protect yours in the e-book Emotional Survival Guide (see Chapter 13).

But before you can fully benefit from the work in this workbook, you will need to unlearn your old learning patterns and replace them with new ways... what I like to call Positive Learning.

What is Positive Learning?

To learn all this new information, which might test your beliefs or make you question the efficacy of these techniques, you may need to change your beliefs around how you learned in the past.

Why Would You Be Interested in Positive Learning?

I've taught toddlers, children, young adults and adults all my life. I've taught English language skills to non-English speakers, drama and performance skills, career transition and interview performance skills and spiritual development. I've taught formally in a classroom and education system and informally as mentor and workshop facilitator, and I've learned a lot about how we learn and how we feel when we learn new things... and it's always perplexed me.

Even someone like myself who loves learning as much as teaching has had issues with learning new things. There is anticipation, excitement and underneath that, fear of failure and anxiety. I've learned to push through these feelings but the problem with having negative responses to learning is that it blocks our learning abilities and in particular, positive emotional responses to learning.

I've met many clients who have been immobilised with fear at learning, refusing to allow themselves a new position suited to their talents because the fear of becoming certified has stopped them progressing in their career. When my clients have ventured into their learning issues, it is always rooted in one of four responses learned around 4 years of age that is then consolidated over the coming years into negative beliefs about their ability to learn.

These are:
  1) **Fear of learning** – often passed on by a parent's experience.
  2) **Pain** – the bad experience of learning results in emotional, mental (and in some cases, physical pain – I see this in adults who were punished physically because of their test results etc.).

3) **Comparison** – the whole concept of testing and comparing one student against another denies the child the natural right to believe it has come here on earth to express its core gifts. Comparison shuts down collaboration and damages the child's natural desire to contribute and give freely of their talents.

4) **The shame of failure** – if this happens too often, the child refuses to learn, has a fear of learning, develops low self-esteem that can filter into all parts of their life, and seeks only to find safety, which by its very definition limits the person. All of these responses keep us stuck, unable or unwilling to engage in learning and life.

*If a child naturally learns through play,
laughter, joy and love, how is it helping us as adults to
learn through fear, pain, comparison and failure?*

I took this question to my angelic guides for an answer and they replied:

"It isn't! It's detrimental to humanity's existence on many levels. You are starting to fear your creation of artificial intelligence because you fear they will overcome your highly-prized skills of data memory and creating solutions from what you've known in the past.

But this is erroneous thinking, if you create from the past, you will create a future based on it. This denies and limits the creative capacity of thought. All of your recognised geniuses have begun with articulating a problem and then allowing their minds the freedom to be inspired by everything around them to shape theory and then use the knowledge they have to prove its veracity.

At a more elementary level, the people you consider geniuses in their field have become so because their true talents have had the space to shine. They have worked hard but they've maintained their childlike laughter, glee, joy, playfulness and love to focus their attention on their talent, and it has blossomed in multiple directions, bringing benefit to the whole of humanity.

You consider this genius as unique, special, almost a freak of nature, if you will, but this is possible for all human beings – even those you consider to have a disability still come with unique gifts to share into the world – but your view of society and education has limited that potential.

Over the next decades, the education system must be overhauled and in particular, your way of categorising humans must cease or you will educate yourself out of existence.

For those of you thinking "what has how you feel about learning got to do with life?" we say this:

EVERYTHING! *Because your life is about constant learning moment to moment. Most people would not agree with this statement but this is because you've created a living reality that limits how you see learning and tends to put formal learning on a pedestal.*

Mostly, your learning is through living life and your formal learning confirms what you already know! The truly dynamic learning space is in life. You are designed as a biofeedback system, therefore, if you do not have the tools to experience the new information that is swirling around in your energy field (because you're emotionally stuck in fear, pain, comparison or failure), you will die before your time, before you've delivered your unique contribution to the world, and before you've been a benefit to society.

But imagine for a moment what you could achieve if you stayed in the vortex of childlike laughter, glee, joy, playfulness and love?

  I. How open would your life be?
  II. How much more alive would you feel?
  III. How much more energy would you have? How many more options would you find to a problem that's perplexing you?

The answer is… limitless! This is the place for creativity and intuition to thrive and what is needed as humanity grows into the next level of humans' 'being'.

So we ask you to please take part in this shift from the old conditioning of fear to reclaiming your childlike wonder and glee in positive learning."

SESSION # 1 - INSTRUCTIONS
This session is about your attitudes toward learning. It comes in 2 parts.

Part 1 is a chance to review all the old patterning, thoughts and beliefs you have about how you learn. What your parents, teachers, siblings and peers taught you by their judgements of your learning skills and your emotional responses to them. Write as many of your memories down and number each one. Look at how you feel, where the feelings sit in your body and what response you give to others' judgement of how you learn.

Once you have as full a list as possible, get a red pen or marker and put a line through everything you have written down. Put crosses next to each statement and give yourself a zero out of the total number of examples you've given, e.g. 0/20. (This is important to do as marking your work is one of the ways you were judged, corrected and shamed for your learning and lack of memory to recall and regurgitate facts.)

Part 2 is a series of statements you will need to say aloud.
These statements are a guide only. If you wish to choose your own words, then do so. We suggest you say them aloud, so your body can hear you asking for this release.

- The space between each statement will be up to you.
- You will know when you need to move on to the next statement.
- Trust your intuition. You cannot do this exercise incorrectly.
- We suggest you take your time.
- You may want to release the pain, fear and shame of your previous learning and allow yourself to learn in joy and curiosity.
- You may have tears and unexpected emotions; honour these and do what feels right.

Record any impressions that are important to you, but remember that the reason for this attunement is to let go of the pain, not hold onto it, so if you have no idea what the specifics of your release are about, don't worry.

Before you begin:
1) Switch off all phones etc. You need to be free from interruptions.
2) Light a candle asking for the light to come in and protect you.
3) If you use anything else – crystals, aromatherapy, music, etc. – do what you feel comfortable with.

Part 2 of the session begins now:

1) "I ask for protection from my guides and angelic realm through this session and beyond."

2) "I see my being and where I am right now surrounded by unconditional love gently supporting my actions."

3) "As I breathe in easily and effortlessly, I visualise my lungs and see the pain, sorrow and sadness locked into my lungs… my physical body may respond to this visualisation but throughout this process, I am safe and whole."

4) "I watch now as my healing angels and guides work to soften and dissolve this energy, releasing where I am frozen into fluid and then to air all feelings of grief and shame around learning new things…"

5) "I release my pain, sorrow and shame from this lifetime… I accept that it is time to let this emotional baggage go."

6) "I let go of the need to compare myself to others and compete with them. I have come to Earth to express my unique gifts, talents and creativity and I allow myself the opportunity to shine my very best into the world."

7) "I choose to collaborate with others, to add my skills to those of others so that the perfect holistic result is achieved."

8) "I see failure as part of the process of creating the right experience. I embrace failure as a step on this road. I let go of fear and shame around failures from the past and for any that may occur in the future."

9) "I choose to be curious about life around me, to create with the understanding of the balance of nature. I look to all of my actions and continuously choose what is in alignment with and protective of Earth's diverse balance."

10) "I release the grief, sadness and sorrow found in my cellular memory of all negative forms of learning. I hold in my heart the space for peaceful co-existence and loving kindness to all species and parts of the universe. I let go of the fear programming that I came with at birth and I allow the light of love to fill all my life and interactions with this wondrous planet and universe."

11) "I choose to be playful, open to learning new things, willing to change and grow to bring forth the very best of myself into the world."

12) "I embrace my imagination, my intuition and my intelligence to create a world that brings joy to myself and others."

13) "I understand I am a limitless being and that includes my ability to learn and grow."

14) "As I release, I see the energy flowing more easily. The grey whiteness of a frozen landscape is now being awakened by the sun and warmth. My lungs feel free and light and I breathe deeply and easily. My lungs and rib cage opening easily and effortlessly. I am independent and free."

15) "Divine Healing Intelligence, thank you for this healing release and guidance."

To close and protect you after this session:
Place one hand on your head and one on your heart and say aloud:
"Ground – Align – Connect – Protect – Seal – Energise – Balance."
Take a deep breath in and out.

Message from the Angels:
"Beloved, we thank you for the work you have done. We ask you to take your time, be gentle with yourself for the next few days and make notes of what comes up for you. Always with our love and blessings…

The Angelic Realms, Guides for the Awakening and Spirit in its many forms."

POST Session:
1) Rehydrate. These sessions use a lot of your electrical energy and so you need to replenish that by drinking water and lots of it.

2) Reintegrate. If you feel a bit "spacey" after the session, then use Bach Flower Rescue Remedy as per the instructions on how to use these essences. This will help with the reintegration process.

3) Rest. Take it easy. Spend some downtime without technology for a few hours. Go to bed early.

4) Reflect. Make notes of anything that comes into your thoughts or feelings over the next couple of weeks. Share with your friends, if you wish.

CHAPTER 5

* * * * *

Dealing with Loneliness and Isolation

There is no doubt that mental and emotional distress can isolate you and make you feel lonely. Of course, the reality is that the more you feel isolated and lonely, the more likely you will also feel anxious and depressed. It is a vicious cycle.

In the article The Growing Problem of Loneliness, written by John T Cacioppo and Stephanie Cacioppo, it states:

"Imagine a condition that makes a person irritable, depressed, and self-centred, and is associated with a 26% increase in the risk of premature mortality. Imagine too that in industrialised countries, around a third of people are affected by this condition, with one person in 12 affected severely, and that these proportions are increasing. Income, education, sex, and ethnicity are not protective, and the condition is contagious.

The effects of the condition are not attributable to some peculiarity of the character of a subset of individuals, they are a result of the condition affecting ordinary people. Such a condition exists—loneliness."

This article appeared in The Lancet, February 03, 2018:
www.thelancet.com/journals/lancet/article/PIIS0140-6736(18)30142-9/fulltext

I am not surprised by this article. As a counsellor and life coach specialising in mentoring people who wish to live a happy life, I deal with this problem daily. It is the main motivation for poor relationship choices and people staying in relationships that are toxic and unsupportive. Many addictive behaviours can be attributed to it and I know many clients of psychic phone lines call because of loneliness as their number one problem.

When the medical profession realises loneliness is a major contributor to world health in the western world, you know the statistics that are being banded around are only the tip of the iceberg.

I believe loneliness is:
  i) Being unable to communicate things that seem important to you and feeling these or you are unaccepted and unacknowledged by someone who you consider is important to you.
  ii) To not be seen fully, respected, and acknowledged for who you truly are (without masks) by a person important to you.
  iii) The distress caused by the gap between your personal ideal about your relationships and the perceived social relationships you're having.

Loneliness results from feeling:
- Abandoned
- Betrayed
- Condemned
- Denied
- Unworthy
- Unloved
- Misunderstood
- Ostracised
- Isolated
- Not belonging
- Alone
- Unseen/unwitnessed
- Unrecognised
- In meaningful relationships with others.

All kinds of relationships can be impacted by loneliness.

- Grandparents
- Parents
- Aunts/uncles/cousins
- Siblings
- Friends
- Romantic partners
- Career
- Land of birth
- A memory of the land of soul's greatest happiness
- Places
- Seasons
- Society
- City
- Country
- Talents
- Soul
- Religion
- Animals
- Plants
- Devas/Spirit Beings/Angels
- Planetary Soul groups/Soul family
- Soul mate

These 3 sessions I have included here are to assist you with the feeling of loneliness and isolation.

INTRODUCTION:

When you come into this life experience on Earth, information is coded into your DNA at a cellular level. This covers more than your physical abilities and intelligence; it also covers your emotional and mental well-being and ability to cope with the experiences of life. This information remains dormant until triggered by an event or experience. As an adult, you have a choice as to how you respond emotionally, but as a child, you will respond instinctively, and those responses will either be encouraged or denied by parents or caregivers. The responses of our family, friends or important role models impact greatly on our feelings of being supported or feeling alone, and from an early age, we will know if we are supported or not. It only takes 3 repeated emotional responses for a pattern to emerge and a belief about yourself to be established.

All emotions that are the result of trauma or continuous repetition are trapped in the body's cellular memory through the breath. In this instance, continuous repetition refers to the mind-tapes that continue to press upon soul wounds and trigger emotional responses. If these repetitions are not released, they will alter the brain's synapses and become so ingrained as to be considered a reality for that soul.

Once your reality has been established, you bring in experiences that reflect that understanding. There are some key times in your life when there will be a chance for change – these are transition times such as puberty, childbirth (for either parent) or menopause. Other times might be transitions; from school to university to first job or retirement. It is these realities, beliefs and vows you will be releasing as part of these sessions.

Over 3 sessions, you will release all the points in your body and psyche that are triggered to feel disconnected, unloved and lonely… and then you will build new connection points to strengthen your unique sense of self in the world and allow yourself to be free of this feeling and fear. So, let's begin.

SESSION #1 - INSTRUCTIONS
Session # 1 will deal with the loneliness locked into 2 heart chakras. The first chakra you will know as the Heart Chakra – its energy point is the heart, and it is represented by the colour green. It covers all meridians, plus the organs of the heart and lungs. Lungs store grief and love that has not been given, supported, received, or connected. The second chakra you may not know about. It sits on the top of the diaphragm in a narrow band. This chakra I call God's Heart** – it connects to the heart and lungs, all meridians, all bodily systems, and the pituitary gland. It is the part of you that deals with accepting Spirit as a force for good in your life. (Whether you believe in God or not, you will still have this energy point. Another way of understanding this point is to say it's the highest love consciousness.)

** When this is active, you see God in everyone. It activates the energy of loving kindness and compassion for self, others, the planet, and the universe.

Below are a series of statements you can use to take part in the Release Loneliness Session.

- They are a guide only. If you wish to choose your own words, then do so. As previously discussed, there is power in your voice, so I recommend you say them aloud so your body can hear you asking for this release.
- The space between each statement will be up to you. You will know when you need to move on to the next statement.
- I suggest you take your time.
- You may want to release these emotions with tears, or yawns – do what feels right.
- Begin by writing out your points of loneliness from the list given above. What do you resonate with? How would you express loneliness for you? Which statements have the greatest charge for you? You are not being asked to judge these, there are no right or wrong answers, just what you feel.
- Record any impressions that are important to you, but remember that the reason for these healing sessions are to let go of loneliness, not hold onto it, so if you have no idea what the specifics of your release are about, don't worry about it.
- You will complete the whole process with a specific hand massage. The hands are where we hold, give and express love. They hold an enormous amount of emotional content and like the feet, all meridians are held in the hands, so when you massage the hands, you are massaging the body. Make this a quiet, gentle act of self-care. Use a favourite cream or oil to massage into your skin from wrists to the tips of your fingers. Enjoy and welcome this act of self-love. You may want to do this process at other times over the next 3 session times. Do what feels right and good.

Before you begin:
- Switch off all phones etc. You need to be free from interruptions.
- Light a candle, asking for the light to come in and protect you.
- If you use anything else – crystals, aromatherapy, music etc. – do what you feel comfortable with.

The session begins now:

1) "I ask for protection from my guides and angelic realm through this session and beyond."

2) "I see my being and where I am right now surrounded by unconditional love gently supporting my actions."

3) "As I breathe in easily and effortlessly, I visualise my lungs and see the grief, sorrow and sadness and loneliness locked into my lungs... my physical body may respond to this visualisation but throughout this process, I am safe and whole."

4) "I watch now as my healing energies work to soften and dissolve these feelings, releasing where I am frozen into fluid and then to air all the feelings of loneliness I no longer need..."

5) "I release my own loneliness from this lifetime... I accept that it is time to let this loneliness go."

6) "I release all loneliness that I have held (read your list aloud)."

7) "I release the loneliness I have gathered around me that I have taken on from others (read out your list if it applies – if not, the statement is enough to clear anything you do not recognise)."

8) "I release the loneliness I have felt as a result of my choices and reactions to others through greed or ignorance that has meant I have treated other beings in a disrespectful or arrogant manner. In all interactions, I am filled with gratitude and respect."

9) "I release the loneliness I have felt for the degradation of Mother Earth and her abundant life forms, be that of the air, sea or land. From this moment forward, I choose to be aware of how my choices impact on the planet and take every action to make my footprint as light as possible. I know I am always connected to Mother Earth."

10) "I release the grief, sadness, sorrow and loneliness found in my cellular memory of all forms of planetary destruction, war, or desecration. I hold in my heart the space for peaceful co-existence and loving-kindness to all species and parts of the universe. I let go of the fear programming that I came with at birth and I allow the light of love to fill all my life and interactions with this wondrous planet and universe."

11) "As I release, I see the energy flowing more easily. The grey whiteness of a frozen landscape is now being awakened by the sun and warmth. My lungs feel free and light and I breathe deeply and eas-

ily. My lungs and rib cage opening easily and effortlessly. I am independent and free."

12) "Divine Healing Intelligence, thank you for this healing release and guidance."

Hand Massage:
   i) Using your thumb, gently rub the inside of your wrist in a rhythmic, circular motion.
   ii) Then moving from the wrist, move gently along the outer edge of your thumb to the tip – always gently and always in a circular motion.
   iii) Rubbing your thumb between your thumb and first finger of the other hand.
   iv) Continue in this manner until all the fingers and hand are massaged, always beginning with the wrist as the starting point. This way, the front and back of the hand will be massaged as well as the fingers.
   v) When you have completed the tip of each finger, imagine you are pulling out all the stuck energy from the finger and flick it into the air at the edge of your aura (this usually sits at the length of your open arm).
   vi) When both hands are completely massaged, shake them gently and then let them rest.

To close and protect you after this session:
Place one hand on your head and one on your heart and say aloud:
"Ground – Align – Connect – Protect – Seal – Energise – Balance."
Take a deep breath in and out.

SESSION #2 - INSTRUCTIONS
Session # 2 deals with the loneliness locked into the Throat Chakra and the 3rd Eye Chakra. The Throat Chakra's energy point is the throat and neck, and it is represented by the colour blue. It covers all meridians of communication, plus the organs of the throat, mouth, and neck. These points store grief and love that you have not expressed for yourself or others. It stores anger and pain when others have treated you badly and you have not expressed your anger or pain to them. If you have been in relationships where you have been "gagged" or been unable to speak

your truth, then these chakras will hold the energies of isolation, being ridiculed, demeaned or belittled or bullied, and the pain associated with these energies. If you have had a series of relationships that have treated you in this manner, you will have closed the throat down and swallowed your feelings to maintain peace. This brings on feelings of isolation and loneliness or of feeling disconnected.

The 3rd Eye Chakra is the centre of intuition and your ability to pick up when you are in danger or need to take action that may be inspired to help you with your Soul's mission. Generally speaking, you nor your family know exactly what your Soul mission is and often, you need to step outside of the family beliefs to fulfil it. This can cause friction between you and family members, giving you a sense of not belonging, being different or isolated. As a result, you may decide not to trust your intuition, and this disconnects you from your Soul's mission and Source.

There are pandemic signs of this in our world when you look at the number of people dealing with mental disorders and depression. When a soul cannot express itself or connect to the greater Source to find out what it needs to do, then the soul will feel lost, disconnected, lonely and depressed. Clearing out old beliefs, thoughts, and emotions in these two chakras enable the soul to find clearer ways to connect with Source, find answers and express the truth according to the individual soul.

- Below are a series of statements you can use to take part in the Release Loneliness Session. They are a guide only. If you wish to choose your own words, then do so. As previously discussed, there is power in your voice, so I recommend you say them aloud so your body can hear you asking for this release.
- The space between each statement will be up to you. You will know when you need to move on to the next statement.
- I suggest you take your time.
- You may want to release these emotions with tears, or yawns, do what feels right.
- Begin by writing out your points of loneliness from the list given above. What do you resonate with? How would you express loneliness for you? Which statements have the greatest charge for you? You are not being asked to judge these, there are no right or wrong

answers, just what you feel.

- Record any impressions that are important to you, but remember that the reason for these healing sessions are to let go of loneliness, not hold onto it, so if you have no idea what the specifics of your release are about, don't worry about it.

- You will complete the whole process with a specific hand massage. The hands are where we hold, give and express love. They hold an enormous amount of emotional content and like the feet, all meridians are held in the hands, so when you massage the hands, you are massaging the body. Make this a quiet, gentle act of self-care. Use a favourite cream or oil to massage into your skin from wrists to the tips of your fingers. Enjoy and welcome this act of self-love. You may want to do this process at other times over the next 3 session times. Do what feels right and good.

Before you begin:
- Switch off all phones etc. You need to be free from interruptions.

- Light a candle, asking for the light to come in and protect you.

- If you use anything else – crystals, aromatherapy, music etc. – do what you feel comfortable with.

The session begins now:
1) "I ask for protection from my guides and angelic realm through this session and beyond."
2) "I see my being and where I am right now surrounded by unconditional love gently supporting my actions."
3) "As I breathe in easily and effortlessly, I visualise my lungs, throat and 3rd Eye Chakra and see the grief, sorrow, sadness, anger and loneliness locked into my lungs, throat and 3rd Eye… my physical body may respond to this visualisation but throughout this process, I am safe and whole."
4) "I watch now as my healing angels and guides work to soften and dissolve this energy, releasing where I am frozen into fluid and then to air all feelings of loneliness I no longer need…"
5) "I release my own loneliness from this lifetime… I accept that it is time to let this loneliness go."
6) "I release all loneliness that I have held (read your list aloud)."

43

7) "I release the loneliness I have gathered around me that I have taken on from others, (read out your list if it applies – if not, the statement is enough to clear anything you do not recognise)."

8) "I release the loneliness I have felt as a result of my choices and reactions to others through greed or ignorance that has meant I have treated other beings in a disrespectful or arrogant manner. In all interactions, I am filled with gratitude and respect."

9) "I release the loneliness I have felt for the degradation of Mother Earth and her abundant life forms, be that of the air, sea or land. From this moment forward, I choose to be aware of how my choices impact on the planet and take every action to make my footprint as light as possible. I know I am always connected to Mother Earth."

10) "I release the grief, sadness, sorrow and loneliness found in my cellular memory of all forms of planetary destruction, war, or desecration. I hold in my heart the space for peaceful co-existence and loving-kindness to all species and parts of the universe. I let go of the fear programming that I came with at birth and I allow the light of love to fill all my life and interactions with this wondrous planet and universe."

11) "As I release, I see the energy flowing more easily. The grey whiteness of a frozen landscape is now being awakened by the sun and warmth. My lungs feel free and light and I breathe deeply and easily. My lungs and rib cage opening easily and effortlessly. I am independent and free."

12) "Divine Healing Intelligence, thank you for this healing release and guidance."

Hand Massage:

  I. *Using your thumb, gently rub the inside of your wrist in a rhythmic, circular motion.*

  II. *Then moving from the wrist, move gently along the outer edge of your thumb to the tip – always gently and always in a circular motion.*

  III. *Rubbing your thumb between your thumb and first finger of the other hand.*

  IV. *Continue in this manner until all the fingers and hand are massaged, always beginning with the wrist as the starting point. This way, the front and back of the hand will be massaged as well as the fingers.*

V. *When you have completed the tip of each finger, imagine you are pulling out all the stuck energy from the finger and flick it into the air at the edge of your aura (this usually sits at the length of your open arm).*

VI. *When both hands are completely massaged, shake them gently and then let them rest.*

To close and protect you after this session:
Place one hand on your head and one on your heart and say aloud:
"Ground – Align – Connect – Protect – Seal – Energise – Balance."
Take a deep breath in and out.

SESSION #3 - INSTRUCTIONS
Session #3 deals with the loneliness locked into the Divine Feminine and the Divine Masculine Chakras, which sit between the root chakra, the sacral chakra and the heart and throat. They are part of the 5th-dimensional higher-being chakras we are adapting as we become more in alignment with the new earth.

Both these chakras have their energy point on the spine and it will be opposite, depending on what sex you have chosen to be this time. If you are expressing as a woman, you will have the Divine Feminine (pink) on the Lumbar 4 and the Divine Masculine (coral) on the Thoracic 3. If you are expressing as a man, they will be reversed, i.e. the Divine Masculine (coral) will be the Lumbar 4 and the Divine Feminine (pink) will be Thoracic 3. The reason for this is the 5th-dimensional chakras spiral the body rather than sit in a direct line from the crown to the root chakra, as in the 3rd-dimensional chakras.

The Thoracic 3 represents your wisdom, inner guidance, intuition, trusting yourself rather than others and expressing who you truly are.

The Lumbar 4 represents your empowerment on all levels. It covers your clarity in the physical form, knowing your purpose and acting from the soul perspective rather than the ego. It's about valuing yourself and feeling worthy. Much of the world disturbance you can see reflects this lack of worth and trust in yourselves and your unwillingness to accept full responsibility for your responses and the consequences of your actions. You have been led to believe that others have the power, not yourselves, but for the divinity of your true souls to shine through, you need to understand that you are the power. You are co-creators of your world and you can and must make the changes to rebalance yourselves. When you do this, the earth will rebalance naturally. You do this by living from a loving heart.

The loneliness you feel at this level is the sense of disconnection from your higher being (or soul) and the love of Spirit and the earth you live on. It results in addictive behaviours, lack of joy or enthusiasm, apathy, and depression.

- Below are a series of statements you can use to take part in the Release Loneliness Session. They are a guide only. If you wish to choose your own words, then do so. As previously discussed, there is power in your voice, so I recommend you say them aloud so your body can hear you asking for this release.
- The space between each statement will be up to you. You will know when you need to move on to the next statement.
- I suggest you take your time.
- You may want to release these emotions with tears, or yawns – do what feels right.
- Begin by writing out your points of loneliness from the list given above. What do you resonate with? How would you express loneliness for you? Which statements have the greatest charge for you? You are not being asked to judge these, there are no right or wrong answers, just what you feel.
- Record any impressions that are important to you, but remember that the reason for these healing sessions are to let go of loneliness, not hold onto it, so if you have no idea what the specifics of your release are about, don't worry about it.
- You will complete the whole process with a specific hand massage. The hands are where we hold, give and express love. They hold an enormous amount of emotional content and like the feet, all meridians are held in the hands, so when you massage the hands, you are massaging the body. Make this a quiet, gentle act of self-care. Use a favourite cream or oil to massage into your skin from wrists to the tips of your fingers. Enjoy and welcome this act of self-love. You may want to do this process at other times over the next 3 session times. Do what feels right and good.

Before you begin:
- Switch off all phones etc. You need to be free from interruptions.
- Light a candle, asking for the light to come in and protect you.
- If you use anything else – crystals, aromatherapy, music, etc. – do what you feel comfortable with.

The session begins now:
1) "I ask for protection from my guides and angelic realm through this session and beyond."
2) "I see my being and where I am right now surrounded by unconditional love gently supporting my actions."
3) "As I breathe in easily and effortlessly, I visualise my lungs, Lumbar 3 and Thoracic 4 and I see the grief, sorrow, sadness, apathy, addictive behaviours and loneliness locked into my light body and physical body… my physical body may respond to this visualisation but throughout this process, I am safe and whole."
4) "I watch now as my healing angels and guides work to soften and dissolve this energy, releasing where I am frozen into fluid and then to air all feelings of loneliness I no longer need…"
5) "I release my own loneliness from this lifetime… I accept that it is time to let this loneliness go."
6) "I release all loneliness that I have held (read your list aloud)."
7) "I release the loneliness I have gathered around me that I have taken on from others (read out your list if it applies – if not, the statement is enough to clear anything you do not recognise)."
8) "I release the loneliness I have felt as a result of my choices and reactions to others through greed or ignorance that has meant I have treated other beings in a disrespectful or arrogant manner. In all interactions, I am filled with gratitude and respect."
9) "I release the loneliness I have felt for the degradation of Mother Earth and her abundant life forms, be that of the air, sea or land. From this moment forward, I choose to be aware of how my choices impact on the planet and take every action to make my footprint as light as possible. I know I am always connected to Mother Earth."
10) "I release the grief, sadness, sorrow and loneliness found in my cellular memory of all forms of planetary destruction, war, or desecration. I hold in my heart the space for peaceful co-existence and

loving kindness to all species and parts of the universe. I let go of the fear programming that I came with at birth and I allow the light of love to fill all my life and interactions with this wondrous planet and universe."

11) I release apathy and addictive behaviours on all levels.

12) "As I release, I see the energy flowing more easily. The grey whiteness of a frozen landscape is now being awakened by the sun and warmth. My lungs feel free and light and I breathe deeply and easily. My lungs and rib cage opening easily and effortlessly. My lower back opens and relaxes. I allow my 5th-dimensional higher-being energy to have access to my full body here on Earth. I am independent and free."

13) "Divine Healing Intelligence, thank you for this healing release and guidance."

Hand Massage:

   I. *Using your thumb, gently rub the inside of your wrist in a rhythmic, circular motion.*

   II. *Then moving from the wrist, move gently along the outer edge of your thumb to the tip – always gently and always in a circular motion.*

   III. *Rubbing your thumb between your thumb and first finger of the other hand.*

   IV. *Continue in this manner until all the fingers and hand are massaged, always beginning with the wrist as the starting point. This way, the front and back of the hand will be massaged as well as the fingers.*

   V. *When you have completed the tip of each finger, imagine you are pulling out all the stuck energy from the finger and flick it into the air at the edge of your aura (this usually sits at the length of your open arm).*

   VI. *When both hands are completely massaged, shake them gently and then let them rest.*

To close and protect you after this session:
Place one hand on your head and one on your heart and say aloud:
"Ground – Align – Connect – Protect – Seal – Energise – Balance."
Take a deep breath in and out.

POST Session
   1) Rehydrate. These sessions use a lot of your electrical energy and so

you need to replenish that by drinking water and lots of it.

2) Reintegrate. If you feel a bit "spacey" after the session, then use Bach Flower Rescue Remedy as per the instructions on how to use these essences. This will help with the reintegration process.

3) Rest. Take it easy. Spend some downtime without technology for a few hours. Go to bed early.

4) Reflect. Make notes of anything that comes into your thoughts or feelings over the next couple of weeks.

CHAPTER 6

* * * * *

The Power of Self-Care Techniques

It is your self-care techniques that will help support and build your resilience and emotional wellbeing.

You are building an internal muscle in much the same way you may have built muscles and strengthened your core when working to physically improve your health. In some ways, this may be more important than your physical training because much of the success of your workout physically is impacted upon by your emotional and mental wellbeing.

See these exercises as necessary to build core mental and emotional wellbeing. If you see them as a chore, then they will lose their effectiveness. As a general rule, you will need about 5-6 techniques you can call on in any given moment. Some techniques will suit you better than others. There are 20 here, so you can choose what suits you, and it's important to use them daily, so they become habitual.

Like learning anything, mental and emotional wellbeing needs to be practised daily. This is why the weekly workbooks have been designed the way they have, with repetitive actions to help embed the habit in your lifestyle. Creating habits over the 6 weeks will help you elevate and maintain your mood.

1. The Power of Stopping
This is a superpower. You live in a fast-paced world where you have to multi-task and move quickly to simply keep in the game of life, or so it seems. But there is immeasurable power in slowing down or stopping, especially when it comes to the mind and the emotions.

Slowing down, pausing, or stopping long enough to become conscious of what is happening to you removes you from the unconscious behaviour of automatic response that often causes you stress and difficult experiences. Being slower, more aware, and accurate in your thoughts and feelings gives you the chance to decide in the new moment if your automatic reaction is what you want to do. If not, you get a chance to change it.

So how you do it?
1) Stop all motion or movement you are making.
2) Take a deep breath and release it.
3) Align your heart and soul.
4) Ask the mind to stop talking at you for a moment.
5) Close your eyes… ask yourself - What do I need to do at this moment?
6) Listen to what you feel is right and then act on it.

With practice, this will become a natural way for you to behave whenever you feel stressed or overwhelmed – and with practice, it will become a simple and quick technique that re-aligns you to your true self, where the wisdom of being you in the world sits.

2. The Power of Yawning
It was not until I started working with colour healing that I realised whenever I worked with clients, I would move them to the next step and yawn. Initially, I apologised for seeming bored or sleepy but I was neither of those things, and finally, I could contain my curiosity no longer, so I asked my healing guides what was happening. They advised that to yawn is one of humanity's greatest self-care measures because it has 'magical' properties.

Yawning, if done properly, can release stuck energy from the body and allow new energy to come into that space and clear up the problems, realigning the person being healed to their highest health possible at that moment.

Without knowing, I had been assisting my client to help just by breathing and yawning through the session, and also myself, by making sure I did not hold on to that energy while I was working with them.

51

Once I realised I was an empath, I was very wary of working in a healing capacity because of my ability to absorb others' pain. But in fact, the more I did the healing work, the better I became at making sure my boundaries were clear when I worked with others, and yawning comes up trumps every single time.

These days, I yawn with or without clients present. It's one of the ways I process energy around me. If I walk into a place and start yawning, I immediately know the energy around me is denser than I am. The yawning gives me a physical reminder that I need to maintain and keep my energy clear at all times.

How to yawn…
Of course, there is a better way to consciously use yawning to assist you to find greater clarity, calmness, and awareness.

1) Take a couple of deep breaths. Deep breathing is a sign for your body to release and you will often find that as you let the breath out of your mouth, you naturally fall into a spontaneous yawn. This is the body using the technique involuntarily.
2) On the next breath, breathe into a yawn and let the yawn take over until all the air is expelled. You might find you have a second yawn on top of the first and want to make a sighing noise and stretch your body. These are all signs that the body is releasing old energy.
3) Take 3 slow, focused, mindful breaths, slightly pushing your diaphragm out to the front, sides, and back as you breathe in. This will start to fill the lower part of the lungs and will bring on yawns automatically. When the yawn is complete, you are ready for the next deep breath/yawn.
4) Yawning has some excellent follow-ons such as letting go of anxiety, stress, negative thoughts, and feelings. It increases the blood flow to the cerebral cortex, slowing down activity and enabling rational and clear thought. It brings you into the present moment and opens up the aspect of the brain that induces empathy and co-operation. Physically yawning assists the immune system to function more effectively and lowers blood pressure and fever.

NB – Some people find yawning physically difficult, in which case, breathe in through the nose and out through the mouth.

3. The Power of Acceptance

"If what you resist persists then what you accept dissolves."

This alone could make or break your newly-found practice of emotional and mental wellbeing. I was a late learner of this self-care technique. I wish I had come to it so much sooner! It's so invaluable that I get my clients to try this in the top 5. Accepting what is in this moment is a real game-changer. It is your place of power. It releases you from the push-pull of the past and stops you racing to the future as a way of escaping what is currently happening and... because you are only living in this moment, when you feel pushed by the past or pulled to the future through over-attachment to both, you lose your powerful NOW place. If you don't find a way to be with the now, you are still going to find yourself in a similar difficult position tomorrow.

This is brain training 101. And while it's a challenge, it is possible. I am living proof!

What's required here is awareness. You need to slow the mind's thoughts down so you can sift through them and catch your mind out when it goes on automatic pilot, whispering gibberish in your ear! The steps are to stop – slow down – listen – accept – let go. Remember, your mind is only trying to help and protect you. So acknowledge the good the mind is doing and then ask it to go count sheep for a few hours while you work through what you need to do without the mind trying to organise or self-sabotage you.

4. The Power of Deep Breathing
Most people do not breathe deeply so the lower part of the lungs tend not to get as much exercise as they should, and your breathing is shallow, making it harder to get the best results.

Deep breathing requires you breathe into the lower part of the lung, which naturally pushes out the diaphragm all around the body, stretching the muscles that hold the internal organs, pushing air to the bloodstream and cells and letting the organs know that new oxygen is coming in, which in turn reminds the cells to get ready to expel the poisons they are holding.

Deep breathing is slow and steady. By consciously breathing in through the nose and out through the mouth, trying to expel all the last drops of air, it makes you ready for the next big breath in. If you could work up to 5 minutes x 3 per day, you would see a great benefit from this in terms of mental clarity, emotional calm and creative problem-solving. It's worth the effort!

5. The Power of Tiny Movements
One thing I've learned through all of this work with depression and anxiety is that big and grandiose doesn't work and can't be supported long term. The real trick to finding greater wellbeing is in consistent and committed small steps or even micro-steps taken every single day, and this superpower tip is about tiny movements.

It is common when you start to release energy from your body that you may start to feel pain. It is not that you are not moving, it is that you have been stuck or cramped in a particular pattern of muscle and nerve constriction and the pain is showing you how the movement is coming back into your body. Again, this is a perfect time to gently focus on the place where the pain is, and say:

1) "I accept and recognise you. Thank you."
2) And then breathe deeply and focus the breath into this place of pain. Lean into it. Let the painful place fill with the light and see if by doing so, it loosens and releases. It may take a few attempts.
3) If you can place your hand where the pain is, it may give it extra support to let go, release the severity of the pain and calm down the nerve endings that are registering the pain for you.
4) Say – "I thank you and let you go."
5) By stretching gently and making small shifts along your spine, you loosen up the nervous system and allow more oxygen and blood to flow along and into the nerve endings.
6) If pain persists or gets severe, please see your medical practitioner, physiotherapist or alternative body therapist.

6. The Power of the Body Scan
Imagine you can MRI scan your body with your mind's eye and as you do, your body lights up or goes dark at different points on the body. This

is a bit like what an energy healer does. If they're using clairvoyant skills, they will see light, shadows and colours over the body. If they're primarily clairaudient, they will hear sounds as they scan your body or spiritual guides will tell them what's happening and what needs to be done. If your healer relies on their clairsentient feelings, they will use their hands to scan the body and feel the discomfort on their own bodies. Their bodies are literally relaying your body's irregularities. And rarely, you will find a healer that can smell or taste the dis-ease in your body. By practising this power, you will be strengthening the connection between you and your body, so you can read information and support it to:

1) find the treatment you need, and 2) possibly assist yourself in the healing process.
   i) Always start at the crown of the head.
  ii) Run your hand from the crown of your head, slowly down the body, stopping when the energy feels stuck or stiff. If there feels to be a temperature change or the consistency feels heavy or sticky, these could be indicators of imbalance.
 iii) Hover your hand where you feel the need to stop.
  iv) It's important if you are using this power to not second-guess yourself. Trusting the information is vital to the integrity of your skills and the information gathering you are doing.
   v) If you feel a blockage, bring light in through your body and out through your hand to the place that you feel needs help. If you feel a release or you yawn, then know the energy has shifted.
  vi) Continue until the body is clear.
 vii) After a few attempts of this, you will start to know how your body feels and also be getting used to how the energy flows through you.
viii) This is a gentle way of cleansing and clearing the energetic body and can result in feeling like you've had a massage as you become more relaxed and energised.

NB: You can use this technique to follow anxiety and depression, as often, the body will hold the impact of that congestion in the nervous system. Using a combination of deep, mindful breaths, focus, yawning and energy moving you can move the body into a space of more ease and safety, which in turn allows you to function better. Help is only as far away as a therapist should you wish to get further help.

7. The Power of the Check-In

While the Body Scan was a check-in of your physical energy, the Check-In is a check on your emotional, mental and physical body. You will often find that when you are busy, your energy levels can drop quickly. Maybe you worked through lunch, maybe you had a run-in with a work colleague or felt disappointed or unsupported by someone you had relied on.

These daily shifts and balances impact on your energy field, especially if you are a highly-sensitive person or an empath, and so it is vital to Check-In at least 3 times a day as to whether your energy levels are still high or do they need a top-up.

At one time in my working career, I found myself in a challenging job where I dealt with a lot of passive-aggressive personalities and those who were into blaming and shaming others to manipulate the staff. The only way I could get through that job (before I resigned and found a better position!) was to do a body check whenever I took a bathroom break. I got very efficient at the Check-In with myself and managed to keep my energies at a reasonable level so that I didn't drag myself home on public transport and then curl in a ball comatose until I recovered!

If you find your work situation is the one that is triggering you into depression or anxiety, then try the Check-In. You'll find it in your Weekly Workbooks (Chapter 11).

8. The Power of Meditative Communication

This is a style of communication that you share with another person you can trust, like a good friend. Emotions are contagious. So if you're feeling depressed or anxious and you speak to someone who's also worried or anxious, you can create imaginative scenarios that your mind will think are real because you've spent time discussing it repeatedly. The COVID-19 pandemic is a case in point.

Every time I spoke to a particular client on Skype, she would talk about the number of deaths around the world. She could list them off every week letting me know which countries had increased numbers and which had not. She was literally frightening herself with the statistics she was reading.

To break this habit, I suggested she practice Meditative Communication. It works like this:

The 1st person has to say what they're feeling and then notice something that makes them feel good. Then the 2nd person responds with acknowledging the positive statement and then they say how they're feeling and follow with another feeling that is supported by something they are noticing.

Here's an example:
1st Speaker: I feel really anxious and upset about _____ but as I sit here talking to you, I notice the bird singing in the tree (something good) and that makes me happy and I can relax.

2nd Speaker: Yes, I acknowledge your anxiety and I hear the bird singing too. I'm feeling depressed today because I didn't _____ but I'm watching the dog across the road go for a walk with his owner and it makes me remember than when I go for a walk, I feel better, so I'm going to do that today.

1st Speaker: I can understand you're feeling depressed at _____ and I think a walk is an excellent idea. How about we go for one now?

A few minutes of this type of conversation relaxes the tension of anxiety and depression by acknowledging how you feel and then rather than staying in that feeling, actively choosing to focus on something more uplifting. This allows the mood to change.

For this to be successful:
1) Both parties need to understand how to do this exercise and be willing to do it.
2) This kind of exercise needs time, and the conversation needs to slow down so each speaker has a chance to find the "something good" they are going to focus on.
3) As soon as the energy shifts and both parties start to feel a bit better, you can go to a more normal conversation, but try not to go into the blues or anxiety again. Try and talk about something both of you enjoy and like doing together.

9. The Power to Self-Soothe

Self-soothing can be done in a few ways.

1) You could stop talking to yourself in your Inner Critical Voice and practise speaking as though you were 100% empathic, supportive and gentle with yourself, accepting where you are now and encouraging you to feel ok. Talking you through options that you could try that are different from what you're currently using.

   If you are an auditory learner, then this may work well for you. But by far the most effective way to self-soothe is by touch. Light, gentle, soft and unhurried touch that shows you are caring for your body, heart and mind.

2) If you are lying down then you can touch the face for this exercise. If you are sitting, touch your hands.

3) The touch needs to be very gentle, barely there, soft, and continuous. You can do this with or without music.

4) Check the *Depression Relief Workbook – The Album - Week 5* for a soundtrack you can use for this exercise.

5) Face Touch:

   - Start at the bridge of your nose and the eyebrow. Move your fingers gently to the outside of the eyes, around and under the eye, back up to the bridge of the nose. Do this a few times.

   - Then as you reach the temples, add gentle, circular rotations at the temples and continue back under the eyes up to the bridge of the nose.

   - Now using all the fingers of both hands, move up to the top of your forehead, across to your temples, back under the eyes, and up to the bridge of your nose, resting at the start point between your eyes. Do this action a few times.

   - Starting at the bridge of the nose, go across the eyebrows, down past your temples and follow the line of your jaw into the middle of your chin, up to the bottom of your lower lip and around your lips, back down to your chin and up along the side of your jaw to your temples, back under the eyes and up to the bridge of your nose.

   - Again, moving from the bridge of the nose, move slowly to the temples and across to the ears, circling the ear on the top and underneath the ear, going across to the edge of the eyes and back around until you are back to the bridge of the nose. Do this a few times.

- Then using the first 3 fingers, start at the bridge of the nose and move outward to the temples, gently across under the eyes and cheeks in gentle backward and forward motions down the cheeks to the nose and then lips to the jaw point under the chin, along the jawline to the temples, under the eyes and resting at the bridge of the nose.

- Do this exercise until you feel calm and relaxed.

NB: It's important not to dig or pressure or pull the skin. You are not massaging your skin; you are soothing your mind and emotions through this touch.

6) Hands Touch. The hands hold an enormous amount of stress because we use them so often without conscious thought during the day. But they are more than busy appendages. They are connected to the cardiovascular, nervous, and circulatory systems. They are essential for expressing emotions, particularly love. In my years helping souls pass at death, I have been guided by Spirit to gently touch and massage the hands of those who are passing. This is to help them release their connections to the earth plane and to re-connect with their guides and angels in Spirit. I have also been directed to do this exercise around anyone who has suffered shock or trauma because it releases tension from the soul's emotional and mental bodies and calms their blood pressure and heartbeat.

- Always start at the inner wrist of the hand you are going to touch. Using your first 2 fingers, gently draw circles around the wrist. In this, you are setting the rhythm, so make sure it is calm, slow and gentle. Do this a few times.

- Then using your whole hand, gently capture the outside of the hand (both sides) and wipe your hand the length of the hand, as though you were pulling off a loose-fitting glove. And drop the energy from your hand to the ground. (You might want to yawn with this action as well.)

- Then go back to the inner wrist and circle again before running your 2 first fingers along the edge of the thumb and inside the thumb as though you were tracing around the fingers. Try not to break touch with the skin for this. Don't rush. Steady, soft, continuous movement is best.

- Continue along the outer edge of the little finger and hand and go across to the centre of the wrist.
- You can pause here for a while and then retrace your steps from there to the outer wrist, up the outside of the hand, the little finger, working across all fingers until you back at the inner wrist, circling again a few times and then stop.
- Breathe deeply for 3 breaths. Then do the opposite hand. It doesn't matter what hand you do first, but make sure you have time to do both hands.

NB: It's important not to dig or pressure or pull the skin. You are not massaging your skin; you are soothing your mind and emotions through this touch.

10. The Power of Laughter
Laughter is a superpower and a natural medicine and mood enhancer when dealing with any congested emotions. There are a couple of ways you can do this.

1) Watch funny videos, read joke books, tell jokes, and read aloud in funny accents, do funny walks, make funny faces; OR
2) Join a Laughing Yoga group. Check online for details (see Chapter 13 for details).

11. The Power of Singing Nonsense
Another superpower is to speak in rhyme or sing nonsense songs. A nonsense song is a type of song written mainly for entertainment using nonsense syllables at least in the chorus. Usually, it has a simple melody and a quick (or fairly quick) tempo.[1]

You can choose these by doing a check on YouTube or simply ad-lib a set of words at the moment to your favourite song. Nursery rhymes are also good for this. I got into the habit of singing nonsense songs when I was doing a daily chore, like making a cup of tea or washing my hands. If the rhythm is catchy as well, you can move your body and do a bit of a dance to the song you're making up; you've then got a whole body power to uplift or change your mood.

12. The Power of Your Own Voice

Your own voice is the strongest superpower you have. Let me say that again... Your own voice is the strongest superpower you have.

When you were a baby, you used the sounds your body made to communicate with others and to know you existed. You found out very quickly that when you cried, you got attention. As you grew into a toddler, you also learned you had to please others to receive love and being quiet was one of the ways you did that. Children who have been overtly censored by parents, carers or teachers to be quiet often have blocked emotions, poor self-esteem and lack confidence in some or all aspects of their lives.

Many of my clients have to learn to speak up, to let their voices out, to express who they are, be that in sound or the written word. Humanity suffers from having people who have a blocked Throat Chakra. Much of the anger and aggression that can be seen in the world is as a result of not being heard, validated, or recognised for who they are.

13. The Power of Transcription - using your voice.

Your inner voices, and in particular, your inner critic is often responsible for you feeling unhappy with yourself. One of the ways to give yourself strong, positive and amplified self-talk that supports your wellbeing is to take the meditation transcript and record the meditation in your voice and then upload on your listening device. You will find a selection of meditation scripts included in this workbook. Until recently, I would record these and add them as MP3's, but recently, I realised it would be far more effective if you read and recorded them in your own voice so you can get the full benefit of listening to your voice in a loving, positive way rather than as the negative, inner critic. (See Chapter 11 for details.)

14. The Power of your Inner Cheerleader

"One of the problems humans have is the Inner Critic has had far too much airtime, while your Inner Cheerleader has been silenced."

To help strengthen your Inner Cheerleader's ability to claim airtime, you make a recording of your voice telling you how fabulous you are or a list of personal affirmations you can listen to daily. You will, over time,

completely change the power of your inner critic, not by trying to eliminate it, but by building the voice of your Inner Cheerleader with positive
emotions and directives.

15. The Power of Gratitude and Thankfulness
There is much that has been made of this superpower and many techniques to help you find the things you are grateful for. But the fastest
way I know to get into the gratitude and thankfulness superpower is to
thank or bless everything that passes your way. And I mean everything.
The good, the bad and the downright horrible! Find a way of doing it in
each moment and give thanks with a simple "thank you and bless you".
It is such a powerful mood changer.

You can't be depressed when you're focused on thanking people, because
you're interacting with people, you are not in yourself. Having said that,
I tend to thank every part of me, even those parts that are in pain or
criticising me. My favourite thank you is to my inner critic.
The inner critic always speaks in absolutes. So, when it's made a statement I say, "I absolutely thank you for pointing that out to me. I know
you're only trying to help, BUT I'm going to try something different and
I'd appreciate if you would give me a few minutes to try this _____
(whatever it is that you're trying to do). Go take a rest and I'll call you
back if I need you, ok?"

And if I can't find a positive statement or my self-awareness goes AWOL
then simply saying "thank you" three times seems to do the trick. Remember, a lack of gratitude is often because we're running at life rather
than taking time to "smell the roses".

16. The Power of Writing a Journal
Again, there are many ways this can be done and there are as many
books and blog posts out there to show you how it can be done. The
Artist's Way by Julie Cameron is one of the best for creative types. But,
before you rush to learn this new method, start with something simple.
Ask yourself if you like to write things down. Are you a note-taker? A
list maker? A writer of any kind? If you are – go ahead.

This superpower is yours. BUT if it's a trial, a chore, worse than having
your fingernails pulled out with pliers and no anaesthetic, then let this

go. It isn't your superpower and its ok. There will be something else you can do instead.

17. The Power of Commitment to a Daily Practice

Especially when you are beginning something new or challenging, it may take a while for you to master it. I studied singing for 15 years, and while I was more than proficient at it – practiced even, in certain situations, as I had been a professional performer – it took many years of dedicated commitment to the daily practice of singing, scales, correct breathing techniques, body warm-ups, physical exercise, learning new roles, languages and movement before I could say I was proficient.

Mastery is a moving target I've found. Mostly, I did it with joy, but some days not so much. After a while, the rigour of daily practice beginning with 30 minutes and working up to 2-3 hours a day (depending on if I was performing or not) became the norm. It is the way you live your life.

Now, years later, I no longer sing, but I do write… and I write every day. The power of commitment to daily practice, a little every day, has again become who I am. The discipline once learned can be applied to all parts of your life, and I have made this commitment to my emotional and mental wellbeing as well.

18. The Power of Meditation

Meditations are an excellent way to realign your soul, etheric bodies and your physical self. They help you build a self-awareness and mindfulness practice, both of which can help with managing your emotional wellbeing. There are many options on YouTube or phone apps.

I would, however, caution you to not forget to the 7–Step Ground-In because meditation takes the mind away from the other parts of your being and it needs to be re-grounded into your body after the meditation process is completed, otherwise you are opening your aura to possible negative elements that could make you feel more anxious and depressed.

19. The Power of the 7-Step Ground-In

This is such a useful superpower to have. It keeps you grounded and present in your body and is so simple to use that it is worth the effort to make it a "go-to habit" for emotional and mental self-care.

Place one hand on your head and the other on your heart and say aloud:

GROUND – ALIGN – CONNECT – PROTECT – SEAL
– ENERGISE – BALANCE

Take a deep breath and release out.
Remove your hands.

You will notice a clearer vision and a feeling of being more in your body.
NB: Once you have done this a few times speaking aloud, your body will rec-
ognise this instruction and you will be able to give the command – GROUND
– and the body, mind, heart and spirit will come into alignment instantly.

20. The Power of the Body Wake-up

This is a tapping process that awakens and aligns the body. It's effective
on waking as we come in from the dream state or as a reminder to the
body to become more present during the day, especially after a shock
or emotional disturbance. The body goes offline, so to speak, when you
sleep or when you are forced to by a shocking event, emotional reactions
or mental overload. This is to protect your soul from danger. From your
soul's perspective, your physical body is like a coat. It can be replaced if
it is no longer able to function for the soul's use (this is what death is).

   i) Starting with the collar bone points, tap using the first finger and
      thumb of whichever hand feels most comfortable. Tap the point for
      a few moments.
  ii) Holding the point under your arm with your hand and the other
      hand on the thymus gland, tap the point for a few moments. Then
      switch hands and tap the other side.
 iii) Tap the two points under your breast area simultaneously.
  iv) Tap gently on the tender spots with your fingers simultaneously.
   v) Tap the top of the head and thymus gland.
  vi) Take several deep breaths in and out and relax.
 vii) Again, allow your body to tell you when you have had enough by
      sighing, yawning or stretching.
viii) You will know this has worked if you feel brighter, clearer and more
      connected.
  ix) A diagram of these points is available in Chapter Summaries.

21. The Power of Tapping Away Anxiety

Anxiety will block the connection between heart, mind and body, so having a tapping point you can use to help regulate your anxiety is an essential tool.

i) Before you use the tapping point, take a deep breath into the body.

ii) On a scale of 1-100, how high would you mark your current anxiety (100 being highest, 0 being none)?

iii) Take the first number that comes to you as your mark.

iv) Tap on the anxiety point gently – using both sides of the body.

v) Stop when you feel you have done enough tapping.

vi) Take a deep breath in and out.

vii) Now, what number would you choose?

viii) Keep doing the exercise until you feel comfortable... most people don't do more than 2-3 times.

ix) You will notice that your breathing has calmed and you could then apply The Concertina Breath to deepen the effect of feeling calm.

x) A diagram of this point is available in Chapter Summaries.

CHAPTER 7

* * * * *

Are you an Empath?

Why do you need to know?
The key qualities of Empaths and Highly Sensitive People are:

- Awareness of others' pain – physically, emotionally, mentally and spiritually.
- A desire to alleviate the pain of others by absorbing it from others.
- A highly-sensitive awareness of energetic impulses all around them – remember, we are all first and primarily energy.
- Poor energetic boundaries between oneself and others.

All of which results in empaths taking on the energy of others as if it were their own. This is particularly dangerous if the empath is already carrying a predilection to depression or anxiety. Empaths will always hear comments like "I feel so much better when I've spoken to you!" "I was feeling blue, but I feel so much more positive now!" Energetically, empaths will feel exhausted when in the company of someone who is carrying emotional baggage, even though they may have begun the connection feeling upbeat and happy.

What does this mean to my treatment for depression and anxiety?
- If you're an empath or an extremely sensitive person, you are three times more likely to feel depressed or anxious around certain people or places you visit.
- Once identified as an empath, then you need to ascertain the percentage of depression that belongs to you versus others. You will

always have some depression present yourself as you would not attract it to you unless you did, but if you tested your body through using kinesiology or another form of measuring tool, you'll get a more accurate measurement.

- For example, if on a scale out of 100, you only had 30% of depression and the rest belonged to others, you could release this from your system having some sessions with a kinesiologist.
- From a spiritual perspective, we only have to be responsible for what is ours, not what belongs to others.
- You could try writing out a list of all the places, events etc. that make you feel depressed. If you find that you have more depression that is not able to be pinpointed to an event, situation or a place but is a general feeling of malaise then this is most likely not yours to deal with.
- Then visualise this as:

  i) being put into rubbish bags and being taken to the tip, or

  ii) you could ask your guides and angels to assist in taking it away from you

  iii) making a list on a piece of paper and burning it after its completion

  iv) burying it in the garden

  v) creating a worry jar of dried beans and choosing to put all your depressive thoughts in the jar; then each day, let then go into the rubbish bin so you can start the day with an empty jar

Whatever type of visualisation works, use that. Don't dismiss these techniques as silly or as though they won't work. The mind is very powerful… and these techniques will take hold and be true for your mind if you let them. Up until now, you've let your mind be powerfully negative. What you are trying to do is reverse this trend so it will be at least neutral, if not a positive force in your life.

Working with Depression when you are an Empath
As mentioned before, you will still have to work with moving your depressive thoughts to more positive ones, but just imagine if you could learn to keep stronger boundaries and not need to consider yourself as depressed as you thought. Wouldn't that be a wonderful place to be in?

So… it's time to take the test. You will find the Quiz in Chapter Summaries.

CHAPTER 8

* * * * *

The "Where are you right now?" Quiz

One of the ways to get the space between what you feel and taking actions to improve your situation is through asking questions. This is why many of the exercises in this book are about questioning yourself. Where are you up to? What are you feeling right now? What impacts or aggravates your moods?

These questions make you stop momentarily and re-focus your mind from patterns of negative self-talk to curiosity, to help the mind look for solutions. Of course, you need to then give the mind time to find the answers. When these are in front of you, you can then ask one of the most important questions – *Are these answers true for you right now?*

This is an important distinction to make because a lot of negative and critical self-talk is taken from the past and is no longer relevant to you. It's just that it's had longer to be on repeat cycle and therefore sounds louder and more authoritative to you. The inner critic voice often sounds like a parent, caregiver or teacher who criticised you in your youth.

If the voice in your head isn't telling you the truth for this moment, then do you need to follow through with the negative feeling? Or could you let it go and try a new feeling?

What I've noticed through observing myself and others is that often, the place of pause, the gap between two extremes of feeling, is a sense of nothingness, no feeling or even thought; a stillness that is not necessarily peaceful but isn't peace disturbed either. It can't be measured or named, and this causes a disturbance because humans like to label and box things away. Humans like to either create order or chaos, but they fear "the nothing", the void, the moment of stillness. If you can make friends with this space, you will exponentially improve your life and your responses to it. The void is not really a void; it's a place of a pregnant pause, a place where ideas begin, and a place where you can reach and feel your vastness. It is the very moment of your genius and creativity and your oneness with the Source, God, Allah, or whatever you wish to call the great consciousness. It is also the place of choice, the truth-point of your real power. In choosing, you can focus on an emotion that feels better for your well-being.

What a powerful idea that is… to have control over how you feel and respond to the world around you! You can use this quiz at any time, but it is especially relevant at the following times:

1) Before you begin this workbook. This becomes your start point.
2) After you have completed the workbook to gauge how you've improved your emotional wellbeing.
3) You could also use this quiz at the beginning and end of each day or week. Remember, your moods have a chance to change every 1.5 minutes – that's a lot of moods over the space of one day.
4) Tracking via this quiz allows you to start seeing the patterns in what triggers you.
5) Many of your responses to life's events began much earlier than the now you are dealing with them. This is why it is relevant to ask, "Who was I growing up?"

The Quiz

Part 1 - Who are you now? Basic answers here, please.
- Age
- Gender
- Relationship status
- Current employment status
- Number of children

- Pets in the home
- Do you take alcohol/cigarettes/recreational drugs?
- Do you take prescription drugs – what for?
- Do you go to a counsellor or therapist?
- What's your diet like?
- Do you exercise? How often? When? Where?
- Do you have close friends? Do you meet regularly?
- If you are feeling depressed or anxious, how long have you felt like this? Is there an event that brought this feeling on?
- Where are you living?
- How secure do you feel? In yourself, your life, your financial situation?
- Is there anything you would like to change about where you are right now?
- How do you feel right now? On a scale of 1-10 (1 being low and 10 being high), how are you feeling?

Part 2 - Who were you growing up?
- Did you have both parents in your life?
- Did you have extended family relations – grandparents, aunts. uncles, cousins?
- Did family friends represent any of the extended family relations?
- Did you trust the adults around you?
- If you had a problem or was hurt in any way, was there an adult to help you? Who? How did they help you?
- Did you feel safe, loved, cared for around your parents or caregivers?
- Did you have friends either locally in and around you home or at school?
- Did you have a special or best friend? Or a group of friends?
- What was the singular most important thing to happen to you between the ages of 1-10? 10 -20? 20-30? At any other times? Make a timeline of these things. It can be good or bad events, i.e. move home, leave home, get married, first love, emigrate, etc.
- Have you felt depressed or anxious before? How old were you when this happened? Did you overcome this? How? If you didn't overcome it, how did it develop until now? What are the symptoms of your depression or anxiety? Have you had professional help with this?

- When you think back to the times you have felt depressed or anxious before, can you remember if there was a specific event, person, or trigger to the feeling?
- What triggers you to have an episode now?

Part 3 - How are you feeling right now?

Time and space are constructs of our 3-dimensional world, but we only exist in the ever-present now. The past may be strewn with heartache and regrets, sorrow, shame, and blame. The future is yet to be and you fantasise the future into being by using your thoughts and emotions (whether consciously or unconsciously).

You're filling your future with fear, worry, doubt, projected emotions from the past... why? Because you're holding on to the past in this now, therefore your future can only be a representation of the past struggles you have had.

Sometimes your soul overrides this, to remind you that better options exist or that you can choose to grow rather than contract. But, the way forward is to pick out all the positive times from your past. Times you have been successful, overcome difficulties, believed in yourself. These are important reminders of your ability to create positive realities, to remember you can choose differently to where you're thinking now.

EXERCISE:

i) Make a list of all the good times. This will be a list you can call on to remember when you were successful, happy, or fulfilled.

ii) From your list, choose 3 and write them out in detail. Remembering how you felt, what the weather was like, what were you wearing, who was there with you, what did people say to you, how did your body feel, your heart, mind, etc.

iii) Put it somewhere you can review it for the days when things are not going well.

So, what are you feeling right now?

My clients are always surprised when we dig into this moment, this now. Invariably, they find they are actually feeling ok. Not ecstatic maybe, but not dire. The feeling of things being terrible is the mental tape. Your mental tape is creating stress and depression.

Often, when you stop and pause, you'll find deep inside that you're ok. It is the noise we carry with us that is not ok. This is why the first technique you will discover is the Power of Stopping (see Chapter 6).

You'll have a more immediate experience of this quiz when you take part in the Daily Preparation Quiz.

Where would you like to be by the end of the workbook? How do you think your life might look when you're emotionally healthy? These and other questions you will find when you fill out *My Bucket List* in Chapter Summaries.

CHAPTER 9

* * * * *

PREPARATION *for using*
The Depression Relief Workbook

What to expect over the next 6 weeks?
The next six weeks will help train you into a new way of appreciating your senses, emotional fluidity and expression and learn new tools to deal with the feelings that are being detrimental to your emotional well-being.

But first, you need to…

Make your commitment
Committing is like announcing to your whole being that you are planning to do something different than before and requesting every part of you get on board the bus for the journey to your new self.

Some parts of you will resist. Some will think they already have the answers (especially your mind – be warned!).

What's needed here is a heart and soul commitment. Commitment from these parts of you is aligned more with the truth of who you are and what you want. When you put your heart and soul into something, you get better traction and results.

Commitment means being committed to:
    i. Being curious to find out more about how you feel
    ii. Showing up and doing the work daily
    iii. Being open to change and growth

iv. Failing at the tasks for today but getting back to them tomorrow

v. Keep going for the whole 6 weeks

vi. Accepting all of who you are

vii. Being gentle with you

viii. Honouring all the small steps and "aha's" you have along the way

ix. Not judging you as you have in the past

x. Being patient

xi. Embracing the changes you make to you

xii. Celebrating who you are

I _____, am committed to following through *The Depression Relief Workbook* and following the 12 points as listed.

Signed:

Date:

Creating your Progress Diary

You can create your Progress Diary or simply follow the Weekly Workbook Pages – whatever suits you best.

I've found that my clients tend not to use the workbooks I've created but choose to do their version as this allows them to have a place for extra writing and intuitive responses that may not come when strictly following the workbook. But this is entirely up to you.

How to use the Progress Diary:

1) Use daily.

2) Follow the exercises at the times stated (i.e. morning, lunch and evening).

3) If you miss a day, continue as though you have not missed it.

4) If you miss more than 1 day, go back to the beginning of that particular workbook and start again. Sometimes it will be outside influences that disturb your daily practice and sometimes it will be you self-sabotaging your progress. If it's the latter, please stop what you're doing and check it out. It may be something important.

5) Go to your Preparation Questions to see if you can uncover what your "self-sabotage is hiding". It may be important and require a

session with your counsellor. Don't think of this as a failure. It's excellent news when you discover a stumbling block because you are one step closer on your healing journey.

6) Don't forget to check-in at the end of the week and make a progress report. I cannot stress how important this is. One of the symptoms of depression is being unable to notice small changes and looking for the "big shift" or "great aha moment" all the time, when in fact, better change is incremental shifts that build strength and resilience.

7) No matter how many times you stop, you must start again as soon as you can. The longer you leave between stopping and starting again, the more likely you will give up altogether, and why would you want to fail?

Weekly Workbook

Each week, you will be able to follow the focus and exercises for that week. The workbooks will be available for download from a page on the website www.melodyrgreenbooks.com after you have purchased your copy of this workbook.

Each workbook will include:
- 1 x Weekly Schedule Planner
- 4 pages of exercises associated with each week's sense
- 21 x Daily Check-In Sheets (3 x per day x 7 days)
- 7 x What's My Mood Today?
- 7 x Daily Tracker
- 1 x Mp3 music chosen to connect you to the sense you're working with (see The Album for details)

CHAPTER 10

* * * * *

Weekly Workbooks

How to use *The Depression Relief Workbook* each week
These workbooks have been designed to keep you on target for the coming weeks. Each week focuses on a specific sense, Week #1 beginning with your sense of sight and the importance of colour in your life.

Our senses help us connect and give meaning to our lives. When you suffer from depression, the range of colour and enjoyment in life dims. If you suffer anxiety, you get overwhelmed and panicky about the abundance of your senses, all around you. Both are responses to receiving too much stimulation, too quickly or too often.

Day #1 of the week
1) Download the book for the week.
2) Answer the Daily Preparation Quiz below:
   i. Where are you now?
   ii. How do you feel?
   iii. What support do you need right now?
   iv. Do you know where to get that support?
3) Check to see what you might need to help you with the week so you can be prepared before your start (e.g. the taste week requires you to have different food substances).
4) Choose a Self-Care Technique you will master during the week (see Chapter 6 for details).
5) Fill out the Weekly Schedule Planner – making sure you set time aside in your schedule for this work.

6) Complete What's My Mood for Today?

7) Complete the Daily Check-In Sheet.

8) Listen to the music for this week. How do you feel listening to it?

9) At the end of your day, fill in the Daily Tracker.

Days #2-6 of the week

1) Answer the Daily Preparation Quiz below:

    i. Where are you now?

    ii. How do you feel?

    iii. What support do you need right now?

    iv. Do you know where to get that support?

2) Complete What's My Mood for Today?

3) Focus on the week's theme.

4) Practice your chosen Self-Care Technique for the day.

5) Complete the Daily Check-In Sheets.

6) Listen to this week's music selection.

7) At the end of your day, fill in the Daily Tracker.

Day #7 of the week

1) Answer the Daily Preparation Quiz below:

    i. Where are you now?

    ii. How do you feel?

    iii. What support do you need right now?

    iv. Do you know where to get that support?

2) Complete What's My Mood for Today?

3) Practice your chosen Self-Care Technique for the day.

4) Complete the Daily Check-In Sheets.

5) At the end of your day, fill in the Daily Tracker.

6) Rest and integrate.

7) Weekly Review.

The workbooks are found in Chapter Summaries.

WEEK #1 – SIGHT AND COLOURS – Days 1-7

"I just want the colour to come back into my life. Depression has taken the colour away. My world has gone grey and colourless." – A client

Preparation

NB: If you are not sure about the colours then google them to find out what the colours mentioned below are before you begin.

This week, you will be focusing on colour. You respond to colour through your sight but people who are blind can learn to feel colour according to its vibration. If you are colour blind, you may find it difficult to differentiate between colours and depths of colours.

The official term for colour blindness is Colour Vision Deficiency. It can impair such tasks as selecting ripe fruit, choosing your clothes, and reading traffic lights. It can also make some learning activities more challenging.

If you feel you may have this deficiency, there are tests you can take. Check out: www.colourblindawareness.org for more details.

The colours for this week in order are:

Day # 1 – Black or white

Day # 2 – Red or green

Day # 3 – Dark navy blue or pink

Day # 4 – Blue or orange

Day # 5 – Turquoise or coral

Day # 6 – Violet or yellow

Day # 7 – Magenta or gold

When considering the pair of colours, answer the following:

- Where can you see the colour?
- How do you respond to the colour?
- What does each colour make you feel?
- Which do you prefer and why?
- Progress Diary and Exercises as per workbook.

This week's music selection is Nature Angels by Eitan Epstein Music.

- How does this music selection make you feel? Explain by giving it an emotion.
- Over the week of listening, have you changed your mind about the music?
- Give the music a mark out of 10 (1 = dislike intensely 10 = love this piece!).
- Integration and Weekly Review.

NB: All worksheets you need are included in each week's workbook on Chapter Summaries.

WEEK #2 – SMELL AND AROMAS – Days 8-14
The Muse speaks about Aroma and Taste

"All around you is a mirror. You are a mirror too. Though you are transparent, you accept the illusion of solid mass as you live in the world. You do this so you may gain a grasp on love. For to find love's meaning, its substance, and to experience its fullness is your only goal. You feel for its shape and look for its colour and texture. At the depth of your being, you know that to know love is to know all there is, and you seek this knowledge with far greater striving than you would believe possible if you could but see it from my perspective.

And who am I? I am the Muse of Aroma and Taste. Through me, you learn to smell and taste the love in everything around you. Often, I have been misunderstood, misrepresented, and sometimes missed altogether, such is the power of your fear. I am the subject of temptation, the food of the mind, the tastes of the soul and the aroma of the spirit. Yet to know me, you need to go beyond all that is – to the heart, where all senses dissolve into the power that is love.

Ah! Here I sense your fear. The journey into this paradise is strewn with bittersweet flavours, some long-held within your memory, thought never to be released.

But how can you experience the fresh and fragrant unless your palate is cleared of the old? Purge yourself of the stale, the repeated and putrid for once cleansed with the waters of forgiveness, you may taste anew from the wellspring that is love.

You do not need to gorge yourself, nor be worried about the calories, carbohydrates, or fat here. Love is sinless. Love is pure. Love is profound. Surrender now.

Through your senses of taste and smell, you will reach once more the sublime state of heavenly paradise that is love expressed.
But where do you look for love?

In grand gestures and peak experiences. You make it so hard for yourself. Love is present in the small, the mundane and the ever-present.

Day in and out showing you all and blindly, you turn from these sacred expressions, your eyes heavenward and distant, searching, always questing to see what is plainly right in front of you.

But these musings bring you back… back to the sacred alchemy of love expressed mundanely, through food. Opening you through your senses of taste and smell into love's sanctuary, and here I hope you stay. Not with my stories for they are trifling baubles to please and amuse the eye and to keep your mind from wandering too far from home.

No! I hope that you stay close in yourself, in the warmth of love's embrace, in the paradise of your desire. In love."

An excerpt from "A Tipsy Man Goes Naked – Love Tales and Recipes" by Melody R. Green

I include this here because I believe our senses are designed to enable us to experience more life, love, and emotional satisfaction. When we allow our senses full rein without attaching our stories, judgments and pain to them, they have the chance to open us to our higher expression and joy in living… and isn't that really what we desire most, the richness of experience?

Preparation:
You will need to collect a series of different aromas over this week. These are:

Day # 1 – A piece of fruit but not citrus, i.e. strawberry, peach, melon, mango, etc.
Day # 2 – garlic
Day # 3 – citrus aroma, i.e. orange, mandarin, lemon, grapefruit, or lime
Day # 4 – chopped fresh basil, lavender, or rosemary
Day # 5 – bleach
Day # 6 – coffee
Day # 7 – tree back, i.e. pine, tea tree, cedar etc.

Emotions and aroma
"Our sense of smell is fundamental to humans and was our primary sense in cavemen days to ascertain danger. Animals have a much greater capacity than humans to detect emotions like fear and anxiety or sick-

ness in other beings. But humans with exceptional olfactory skills are highly regarded in the perfume and hospitality industry.

Our sense of smell and taste work together to understand the food we are eating and smelling. As anyone with a cold will tell you, the food seems to have no taste. What they mean is the sense of smell is impaired and so the aromas of the food are missing. The sense of smell is about perceiving the chemicals in the air or in our food. Each sense is a complex interplay of odorants that vibrate and send messages to the brain.

Your earliest olfactory memories of your mother's perfume and the relationship you had with her will colour your response to that particular perfume. For example, if you had a loving and nurturing mother and you felt safe with her and she wore Chanel No. 5, you will associate those feelings with other women who wear the perfume, regardless of whether they are loving or nurturing. Of course, the opposite is also true. If you have a difficult relationship with your mother and she wore lavender, the likelihood is you will intensely dislike the smell of lavender.

Emotional associations then can impact on your responses to certain sounds, aromas, tastes sights, and feelings. As your mind captures every experience you have ever experienced, your body stores those memories, and they can be brought to consciousness with a well-recognised and remembered trigger. This is why trauma buried in your body responds to triggers from your youth you are unaware of unless you stop to process your responses and heal the wounds.

This week's music selection is Ancient Passacaglia by Erick McNerney.
- How does this music selection make you feel? Explain by giving it an emotion.
- Over the week of listening have you changed your mind about the music?
- Give the music a mark out of 10 (1 = dislike intensely 10 = love this piece!).
- Progress Diary and Exercises.
- Integration and Weekly Review.

NB: All worksheets you need are included in each week's workbook on Chapter Summaries.

WEEK #3 – TASTE AND FLAVOURS – Days 15-21
The Muse speaks about The Essentials

"Some ingredients are essential to life. They are foundational ingredients, usually found in most recipes. They are necessary for each moment of your lives to have depth and richness. They are the magical elements of life that create the blueprint of who you are.

If your lives are designed to experience a lot of salt and sorrows, you will crave sweet honey to soothe the palate. If your lives have too much spice, too much change, too much anger and fire, you will crave the soothing energy of water. If you are too green, very healthy and well maintained, you will crave the heat of spice to give you the peak experiences of life, to spark you into new understanding. And if your life is filled with too much sweetness, you will crave sorrows to help temper your good fortune.

Each one of you comes with a leaning to one more than another, and some of you may never move out of the archetypal tension of your opposite; salt-sugar, spice-water, herbs-spice or honey-salt. A fully rounded life will have a mix of all five essentials. There will be health, succulence, lusciousness, depth and spark. These people will shine with life and look beautiful, even if their image is without the most symmetry because their very being is brimming with all that is good and wondrous in life.

If there is one aim to have in your life, it is this: aim for a life well-lived, experiences treasured as memories and no part of your life rejected, but accepted as part of the whole recipe of your life. Then, my beloved, you will have lived. If we together, you and I, have found this great alchemy, each helping the other, I will share your life and you will be the rich thread of my memory.

Remember…

Water gives and maintains life. Herbs support good health. Spices flavour our experiences of life. Salt expresses our sorrows and…Honey sweetens life and makes it worth living."

*An excerpt from "**A Tipsy Man Goes Naked – Love Tales and Recipes**" by Melody R. Green*

I include this here so you can see what you've been holding on to. Are you holding too much spice, salt or sorrow? Or are you holding onto the desire for more sweet, more excitement, more peace or joy? Holding on stops the flow and fulfilment of life.

Preparation:
You will need to have available the following: salt, sugar, a hot spice such as chilli, hot paprika or ground ginger, a green herb such as parsley, or thyme (fresh if possible), honey and a bitter herb such as dandelion, mint, chamomile, chicory, valerian, mugwort or peppermint. Each day, you will focus on one of these flavours. You can take them in any order but below is a suggested order for you:

Day # 1 – Salt
Day # 2 – Sugar
Day # 3 – Hot spice
Day # 4 – Green herb
Day # 5 – Water
Day # 6 – Honey
Day # 7 – Bitter herb or spice

You are to taste these flavours on their own, not with any other food and at least 3 times during the day (your tastebuds change during a day, so this is important for you to find out). Give each flavour a mark out of 10 (1 = dislike intensely and 10 = love the flavour!).

The reason you're being asked to do this is to see which flavours you enjoy or cannot stomach. How you choose will tell you what you are craving in your life. What you love to taste in your life, what flavours your life with happiness.

Emotions and flavours
Again, your sense of taste is such an important life enhancer and memory holder. You can crave tastes from your childhood that make you feel better when you're unwell. When I was a young girl, I used to get bronchitis regularly and I lacked interest in eating food because I couldn't taste it, and as breathing was difficult, I needed food that was easy to eat, swallow and digest.

My mother used to make me chicken vegetable soup and egg custard and it made me feel better. To this day, when I am feeling sick, I will make myself chicken vegetable soup and egg custard for dessert. They give me comfort when I'm not feeling well and I need nurturing and nourishment. Think about what your favourite foods are and why. Add the list to your weekly workbook.

- Progress Diary and Exercises.

This week's music selection is The Science of Breathing by Nazar Rybak.

- How does this music selection make you feel? Explain by giving it an emotion.
- Over the week of listening, have you changed your mind about the music?
- Give the music a mark out of 10 (1 = dislike intensely 10 = love this piece!).
- Progress Diary and Exercises.
- Integration and Weekly Review.

NB: All worksheets you need are included in each week's workbook on Chapter Summaries.

WEEK #4 – HEARING AND SOUNDS – Days 22-28

"Dance wildly with your senses,
Sing at the top of your voice the
Silent Sounds, only your Soul knows...
And joy will be your delirium."

Ruminessence – *A Year of Poetry inspired by Rumi* – Melody R. Green

I include this poem from my collection dedicated to the marvellous Rumi. We're so scared of our senses when they are so important to the fulfilment of our lives, the expression of our souls and the love in our hearts.

Preparation:
This week, you will concentrate on music and the sounds all around you.

- What do you hear at certain times of the day?
- Can you hear children chatter, laugh or play?
- Do you hear the roar of engines, the screech of brakes of trucks and cars?
- Does loud music blare out of car windows?
- Can you hear the sea or water where you are?
- Is it raining?
- What about insects or night noises you can hear? What are they? How do they make you feel?
- For each day of this week, stop and check the noises you hear on waking, during the day and in the evening.
- Which noises do you prefer? What do the sounds make you feel?

This week's music selection is: For Whom the Bell Tolls by Erick Mc-Nerney.

- How does this music selection make you feel? Explain by giving it an emotion.
- Over the week of listening, have you changed your mind about the music?
- Give the music a mark out of 10 (1 = dislike intensely 10 = love this piece!).
- Progress Diary and Exercises.
- Integration and Weekly Review.

WEEK #5 TOUCH – GIVING AND RECEIVING – Days 29-35

"I felt so emotionally and mentally lost and broken that it was painful and hard to find any joy in life. I couldn't bear to be touched or to touch others in case they wanted something I couldn't give them."

– A client

Preparation:

This week, you will focus on touch.

- Do you enjoy being touched?
- Do you enjoy touching others?
- Are you a hugger?
- Do you stand off from others in your own space with clear boundaries?

If at all possible, see about getting a massage this week. If not, then practice one of either of the hand massages mentioned in this book.

Emotions and giving and receiving touch

Our willingness to be touched can be as a result of how we were touched or not as babies and children. Children who were not touched much as a child tend to be less demonstrative as adults.

Cultural expectations of your culture play a big part in how you touch others or whether you are comfortable with being touched and can cause conflict between interracial couples or migrants in their new country.

This is a complex area and, in most cases, requires negotiation, sometimes with a counsellor present. We can learn to be more comfortable with touch, and some therapies can help with this if it is a problem.

This week's music selection is: Ancient Celtic Dream by Mark Wollard.

- How does this music selection make you feel? Explain by giving it an emotion.
- Over the week of listening, have you changed your mind about the music?

- Give the music a mark out of 10 (1 = dislike intensely 10 = love this piece!).
- Progress Diary and Exercises.
- Integration and Weekly Review.

NB: All worksheets you need are included in each week's workbook on Chapter Summaries.

WEEK #6 – FEELING AND EMOTIONS – Days 36-42

"What often happens to performers (those who must repeat-edly excel, be first or at top levels of performance) is they lose the sight of what made them love the music, dance or sport. It becomes about the business of your career, not the joy you found in your talent, and so everything gets lost as a result."

– A client

Preparation:
This week, you will focus on your sense of feelings and how your emotions work. There is no special preparation for this week, but over the last 5 weeks, you have learned more about your other senses and these will help you work out how your emotions feel.

The most important requirement of being able to feel your emotion and monitor your responses to stimuli is to:

- Feel the discomfort.
- Recognise that your anxiety or closing down of your emotions is due to fear.
- Is that fear real?
- Is your mind being truthful in expressing this fear?
- Is the fear in this moment?
- Do you need to flee, fight, or freeze in this situation to feel safe?
- If you flee, fight, or freeze in this now, will you take the next moment to work on those feelings so you can deal with them more quickly?
- Are your reactions appropriate for now or are you reacting in a sim-ilar way to the past?
- How anxious are you?

To answer these questions, you need to slow down, and you do this by stopping and focusing on breathing and applying a superpower. See if you can use the superpower you've chosen for this week. If not, one of the others that you've used before is fine.

- Progress Diary and Exercises.

This week's music selection is: Spiritual Highway by Mark Wollard.

- How does this music selection make you feel? Explain by giving it an emotion.
- Over the week of listening, have you changed your mind about the music?
- Give the music a mark out of 10 (1 = dislike intensely 10 = love this piece!).
- Progress Diary and Exercises.
- Integration and Weekly Review.

NB: All worksheets you need are included in each week's workbook on Chapter Summaries.

CHAPTER 11

* * * * *

Meditation Scripts

Tips on how to record a meditation:

1) Take your time. Allow lots of time between each sentence.
2) Speak clearly.
3) Don't rush.
4) Did I mention take your time???
5) Think about what you want your meditation to do – make you calm or hassled? Relaxed or stressed?
6) Imagine you're talking to a small child, gently and lovingly so that you can get the right emotion into your voice as you record the script.
7) Branch out and make your own meditation and Inner Cheerleader recordings.

Meditation #1

Let's begin by breathing in and out…

Breathing in and out…

Going deeper into breathing and your body as I count 10, 9, 8, 7, 6, 5, 4, 3, 2, 1…

Deeply settling into your body and noticing your body as you sit on your chair or on the floor where you are lying… feel all parts of your body touch the chair or floor…

And feel your body relaxxxxx…

Focusing on your breathing... In... and out... And again... In... and out...

Feel your breath coming into your body... not through your mouth or nose, but through your hips...

Notice how your body feels when you do this...

Notice the small pains and movements as you continue to breathe into your hips...

Your body is showing you where you are holding on...

Holding on to the pain of your childhood...

Holding on from the pain of those who you hoped would love you unconditionally...

But they didn't... and it's ok... Yes, you were hurt but you are fine... you are alive... You are here...

Keep breathing in and out... let your breath feel into where the pain is... and let the breath release the pain for you....

As you breathe into these places of pain, see the breath become light... the colour will change as you breathe the light into the places of pain... the pain will release... and then go....

On the breath in, breathe in the light, sweetly, softly, pink... The pink of love... unconditional... Soothing... Loving...

And on the out-breath... Lettingggg – goooooo...

On the breath in, breathe in the light, sweetly, softly, pink... The pink of love... unconditional... Soothing... Loving...

And on the out-breath... Lettingggg – goooooo...

On the breath in, breathe in the light, sweetly, softly, pink... The pink of love... unconditional... Soothing... Loving...

And on the out-breath... Lettingggg – goooooo...

And surprisingly, your body is starting to feel relaxed... you are starting to feel relaxed... you are more peaceful... calm... At peace...

Breathe in and let the breath leave your body by pursing your lips and blowing the air out until there is none left…

Slowly breathe in again… Your hips are doing the work, but now it's connected to your heart… Your lungs… your chest… Your neck… Your head… Your arms… Your legs… your knees and your feet…

Your whole body is breathing in… oxygen… love… the lightness of being… peace… calm… and every breath out, you are relaxing… yawning away the negative energy until there is none…

Your whole body is breathing in… oxygen… love… the lightness of being… peace… calm… and every breath out, you are relaxing… yawning away the negative energy until there is none…

Keep breathing in more… oxygen… love… the lightness of being… peace… calm… and every breath out, you are relaxing… yawning away the negative energy until there is none…

Keep breathing in more… oxygen… love… the lightness of being… peace… calm… and every breath out, you are relaxing… yawning away the negative energy until there is none…

Your body is feeling good… your feel relaxed… and gently energised…

The pains in your body are leaving you…. They simply float away from you as though they are small wafts of air. Every breath out… slowly floating away.

You feel lighter… brighter… more your true self… I love you… I love you… I'm proud of you… I think you're wonderful… I think you can do anything you set your mind to do… I see you… you are strong… beautiful… calm…clever…

(ADD YOUR OWN WORDS IN HERE)

Breathe in… Breathe out… There is only this now… The past has gone… The feelings from the past have gone… the hurt from the past has gone… you have released it… you can move on now… you can be whole…

Breathe in… Breathe out… and say…

I am at peace…

I am whole…

I am love...

I love me wholly and completely...

I can make new decisions from this moment...

I can choose...

I can love the life I live...

I can make changes if I wish to...

I am strong and powerful...

I am love.

Breathing in and out... and now your breath is lightening... You are coming back from this meditation... You are feeling refreshed... happier... more relaxed...

Coming back now, on my count...1, 2, 3, 4, 5, 6, 7, 8, 9, 10...

Breathe in and out.

Place one hand on your head and one on your heart and say aloud:

"Ground – Align – Connect – Protect – Seal – Energise – Balance."

Take a deep breath in and out and be here.

The end of the meditation

POST Meditation:

1) **Rehydrate.** Meditations use a lot of your electrical energy and so you need to replenish that by drinking water and lots of it.
2) **Reintegrate.** If you feel a bit "spacey" after the meditation, then use Bach Flower Rescue Remedy as per the instructions on how to use these essences. This will help with the reintegration process.
3) **Rest.** Take it easy. Spend some downtime without technology for a few hours. Go to bed early.
4) **Reflect.** Make notes of anything that comes into your thoughts or feelings over the next couple of weeks.

P.S. If you fall asleep while listening to the meditation, this is perfectly fine.

Life Tip!
Make a recording of your voice telling you how fabulous you are or a list of personal affirmations you can listen to daily. You will over time completely change the messaging of your inner critic, not by trying to eliminate it, but by building the voice of your Inner Cheerleader.

Meditation #2 - PEACE MEDITATION
This meditation is to bring peace to your conscious and unconscious being. To call in PEACE, you must first be aware of the peace in your being, so we begin with the breath.

Breathe in Love... Breathe out, Peace...

This is your only commitment for this meditation... LOVE and PEACE.

From the top of your head.

Breathe in Love.

Breathe out Peace.

Across your eyes and the muscles of your face.

Breathe in Love.

Breathe out Peace.

Feel your jaw, throat and neck and...

Breathe in Love.

Breathe out Peace.

Now let your shoulders feel love and peace.

Breathe in Love.

Breathe out Peace

Your spine and chest, your rib cage and organs they protect.

Breathe in Love.

Breathe out Peace.

Your heart, the chambers of your love.

Your lungs, the cups of your grief.

Breathe in Love.

Breathe out Peace.

Your stomach, the holder of your emotions.

Your liver, the seat of your anger.

Breathe in Love.

Breathe out Peace.

Your belly where your hopes sit.

Your reproductive organs where you create from.

Breathe in Love.

Breathe out Peace.

Your arms and hands that hold and give love.

Your legs that move in fear or joy.

Breathe in Love.

Breathe out Peace.

All four planes of your existence.

Connecting you to heaven and earth.

Breathe in Love.

Breathe out Peace.

And see the light of this energy you have now found in your being spread out to those you love.

Breathe in Love.

Breathe out Peace.

Your neighbourhood.

Your state.

Your country.

Breathe in Love.

Breathe out, Peace…

Breathe in Love.

Breathe out, Peace…

See the light of LOVE and PEACE fill the shadows and bring light to you.

Breathe in Love.

Breathe out Peace.

Give thanks for your life and the learning your life has brought to you.

Give thanks to your teachers.

Give thanks for the experience.

Breathe in Love.

Breathe out Peace.

See the light of Love and Peace fill the light more brightly.

You are seeing and recognising the beauty of your soul… Acknowledge this.

Feel the Light of Love and Peace fill you more fully.

You are feeling and recognising the beauty of your soul… Acknowledge this.

Breathe in Love.

Breathe out Peace.

See the world as one… see humanity as one with the earth.

Breathe in Love.

Breathe out Peace.

See the light and shadow of the world being one…

See the wholeness of the world becoming light.

Breathe in Love.

Breathe out Peace.

See Earth as part of the solar system and our sun.

See the sun and solar system and us as part of the galaxy and part of the universe…

Breathe in Love.

Breathe out Peace.

Bring the vastness of love and peace back to you, your centre.

Ground that feeling of love and peace into your being…

Breathe in Love.

Breathe out Peace.

Ground – Align – Connect – Protect – Seal – Energise – Balance.

Now go about your day in Love and Peace.

The end of the meditation

CHAPTER 12

* * * * *

Resources

The 3- Part Support Tools for Depression and Anxiety from Melody R. Green. Details available at www.melodyrgreenbooks.com

1) The Depression Relief Workbook – due December 2020
2) Colour Medicine Cards – due December 2020
3) Emotional Survival Guide for Empaths and Frontline Workers – published May 2020

Other Resources

- **Colour Products**
  Aura-Soma – www.aura-soma.net
  Spirale Colour Therapy – www.spirale.com.au

- **Flower Essences**
  Bach Flower Remedies – www.bachflower.com
  Shell Essences – www.shellessences.com.au
  The Spirit of Woman Essences – www.spiritofwomanessences.com
  Australian Bush Flower Essences – www.ausflowers.com.au

- **Aromatherapy**
  Perfect Potion – www.perfectpotion.com.au

- **Mindfulness Practice**
  ACT Mindfully – https://www.actmindfully.com.au/wpcontent/uploads/2018/01/Dr_Russ_Harris_-_A_Nontechnical_Overview_of_ACT.pdf

- **Mindfulness Meditations and Podcasts:**
  www.christophspiessens.com

- **Laughing Yoga**
  www.coaching.laughteryoga.org

- **Nonsense Songs**
  www.youtube.com

- **Emotional Freedom Techniques (EFT)**
  www.thetappingsolution.com/what-is-eft-tapping

- **Understanding Your Brain and Body**
  Understanding Your Brain https://mayfieldclinic.com/peanatbrain.htm
  Understanding Your Nervous System
  https://www.dummies.com/education/science/anatomy/a-clinical
  overview-of-the-nervous-system/

Let's talk about the Elephant in the Room…
There is no doubt that COVID-19 (Coronavirus) has brought forth
many frustrations, feelings of helplessness and hopelessness as we face
together changes to our way of life as we have known it. No one in Australia or the world has been unaffected by this pandemic. It has changed
the face of many businesses and services.

For the field of counselling, this has meant remote sessions with clients
via Skype or Zoom rather than face to face.

BUT, please let me assure you that Skype and Zoom are ideal digital
formats for counselling and coaching, and other than "a hug and a box
of tissues" that counsellors or coaches may offer face to face, we can do
the work very effectively with a digital platform.

I have many coaching clients from around the world and I usually con-
duct all sessions via Skype or Zoom.

Let's begin with you… Are we the right fit to work together?
My clients are wonderful, unique human beings. They have come to
a crossroads in their journey through life and are maybe struggling to

accept or make changes to their lives. Sometimes they are held back by childhood issues; sometimes they are triggered by issues happening right now – it doesn't matter how they got here, it matters that they are looking for solutions and support.

All my clients want to understand themselves better and are willing to do the work, apply the tools and techniques I offer, to allow them to move into a new way of being with new insights and strategies for living their life more fully.

They are often Empaths or Highly Sensitive People and choose to serve humanity in all they do; as a result, they can suffer from emotional and mental overwhelm that is detrimental to their health and wellbeing and they need effective tools to deal with this.

My clients know there is a better way and are actively searching for some answers.

What do I do?
I give support, guidance and tools so you can get back to your life as quickly as possible, ready for the next step on your journey. The tools I give you make you independent and feel like you have some control in your life and the direction you are going.

Together we:

- Review your beliefs, thoughts and feelings to see if they are real and true for the person you are now and who you want to become.
- Look at your triggers and challenging relationships and behaviours and find ways to change, improve or release the charge these triggers have for you.
- Aim to enable you to be independent and free.
- I work with you – the whole of you – this includes your guides and helpers in Spirit. We work as a team so you can remember just how fabulous you are and have the confidence to shine your brightest light in the world.
- The tools I use help on many different levels and I am a practitioner in the following modalities that can assist you:

- Energy Healer or Tuner
- Colour, Essence and Vibrational Therapist
- Colour Reflexology
- Life Coach
- Career Counselling and Coach
- Life Mentor
- Nutrition
- Author and Teacher

My programs are designed to give you the tools to make you mentally, emotionally and spiritually independent and free.

How did I become a counsellor and life coach?
I have been working professionally in this field for more than 20 years. Like you, I've been on my own healing journey.

Some of the struggles I've faced have been depression, poor boundaries as an Empath, broken relationships and sexual abuse.

Life can be tough, but as someone wise once said, "We're not given more than we can handle", AND when you have come through the pain, what you are left with is the treasures of your life. How you've navigated the cards you've been dealt and won.

I've been collecting tools and techniques to take those steps. And I can share those with you and guide you moving forward.

OTHER WAYS I CAN HELP:
I understand that finances can be an issue for some clients, and to make sure my work is available to as many people as possible, I have a suite of emotional and mental wellbeing tools being launched in December 2020.

1) The Depression Relief Workbook - This book enables you to find the answers for yourself at your own pace, but guided by me. When you follow the book, you are following the course of activities I give my clients when I coach a virtual program (usually 8 sessions). It's the next best thing to having me be with you the whole journey.

AND...

you can always book a one-off call before, after or during your work through the workbook to get extra help if you wish.

2) Colour Medicine Cards - This collection of healing cards are designed to help you increase your emotional vocabulary and move out of stuck or difficult emotions or situations. The answers to most of your discomfort is found within.

These cards have a profound effect if used regularly. They are extra support while working with *The Depression Relief Workbook* or they can be used on their own to help you increase your emotional literacy.

3) Emotional Survival Guide - This e-book looks at boundaries. What happens to yours as an empath or highly sensitive person? How can you strengthen your boundaries so you work more efficiently with others? How do you conserve and expand your energy in difficult situations?

Filled with more than 30 crucial tools to assist empaths to function better in emotionally-charged situations, this book will support you while you're helping others in times of fear and distress.

(This book was written specifically to help frontline workers deal with the emotional fallout of COVID-19 but can be used for all emergencies.)

For further details about these tools, go to:
www.melodyrgreenbooks.com

Acknowledgements

Implementation of cover and interior design: Liam Culver
Cover photo: Unsplash
Back Page Blurb: Carol Chesney Hess - www.carolchesneyhess.com
Editor: Lisa Woodford - www.facebook.com/lisawoodfordbusinesspage

To all my BETA readers for reading and offering suggestions - many thanks for your input. A book like this is not possible without you. I hope I haven't forgotten anyone, please forgive me if I have.

Manufactured by Amazon.ca
Bolton, ON